20-MINUTE
RETREATS
WITH THE
SAINTS

Getting in Touch with Our Desires
for God and Life

DAVID PERRIN

TWENTY-THIRD
PUBLICATIONS
twentythirdpublications.com

> Go to our "Free E-Resources" page
> at twentythirdpublications.com
> to receive three additional meditations

Published in the United States by
TWENTY-THIRD PUBLICATIONS
A division of Bayard, Inc.
One Montauk Avenue, Suite 200
New London, CT 06320
(860) 437-3012 or (800) 321-0411
www.twentythirdpublications.com

ISBN: 978-1-62785-491-7

Printed in Canada.

Contents

Acknowledgements

Anumber of years ago, a colleague, Sam Restivo, Congregation of the Resurrection, approached me about preaching an eight-day retreat for a religious community. He had been asked first, but his schedule did not allow him to accept the invitation. I had never preached an eight-day retreat, which involved 10 talks. I gladly (and perhaps naively) accepted, and the idea of this book – based on those 10 talks – was born. Around the same time, Edward Sheridan, then pastor of Our Lady of Lourdes Parish in Waterloo, Ontario, asked me to assist with Sunday liturgies over the year. Each Sunday, I wrote a homily; from this material emerged a second group of meditations, which contributed additional content to this book. Thank you to both Sam and Ed for providing, albeit indirectly, the events that led to the writing of this book.

I want to acknowledge the artful editing of the full text by Novalis staff Glen Argan and Anne Louise Mahoney. Both made the text flow more smoothly and offered helpful suggestions to improve the text in the editing process. Working with Simon Appolloni, Associate Publishing Director at Novalis Publishing, has been a real pleasure. Under his watchful coordination, everything came together in a timely way.

I would like to thank in a special way the many men and woman – the seekers – who have participated in the various retreats and workshops I have offered in different places over the years. Indirectly, they have contributed to this book; responses to their thoughtful questions and probing comments lie somewhere among the pages you are about to read.

Introduction

How to Read and Use This Book

Historical and Biblical Origins of the Retreat

Taking time away from our regular activities to pray and reflect more intentionally on the presence of God in our lives is a long-standing Christian tradition. It goes back to Jesus himself. When Jesus wanted to reflect on his life with God, he withdrew into the desert, spent time alone in a garden or sought out some other quiet space. He wanted to be alone to listen more carefully to the growing presence of God in his life and respond to the mission that God was calling him to.

Jesus also discerned God's presence and Spirit in his life through his everyday encounters with others. The last three years of his life are recorded in the gospels as a very busy time. He was constantly on the move and encountered people in a range of ways. All the while, through these activities, he became more aware of God's presence.

Jesus' ultimate desire was to respond to God's love, which emerged in his everyday interactions with people. So, from time to time, he left behind his busy life and retreated.

The early Christians did the same; they went out to the desert to pray, or to spend time in a monastery, or simply to sit or kneel alone in a quiet room or chapel, to pray and to listen to the word of God emerging within their lives or through their reflection on the scriptures. Even though the daily activities are filled with God's grace and presence, listening to how this is so requires attentive listening and discernment – and thus some time in silence. In the end, retreats do not take us away from everyday life but insert us more intentionally into it.

Over the centuries, large groups of religious sisters, brothers and priests have made retreats a permanent part of their lives. Some made vows to remain in silence for the rest of their lives so they could pray and listen. A number of these religious congregations continue this mission today, although there are far fewer of them now. Still, the discipline of a retreat remains an important part of the Christian tradition. More and more laypersons make retreats in a range of ways.

The Purpose of This Book

Even if you have never been on a retreat, it's not too late. All it takes is a commitment and desire to explore more intentionally your relationship with God. Essentially, a retreat requires a small amount of time and the desire to learn to listen to God speaking to you through your life experiences.

But what if your schedule, commitments (such as work or family), financial resources, lack of ability to travel or health do not allow you the luxury of leaving everything for a week or even a few days to go on a retreat? No problem: you can do the retreats in this book anywhere, anytime. Simply set aside about twenty minutes, find a quiet space and follow the suggestions in "How to Go on Retreat" (see page 13). You'll soon get into a routine that makes it easy to withdraw from daily life, however briefly. Nothing is carved in stone, and nothing is "magic" about the twenty minutes allotted for each meditation, although they were written with that time frame in mind. Take more time than the twenty minutes if you prefer to read more slowly or more deliberately, or to reflect long and hard on the questions posed at the end of each meditation.

The purpose of a retreat such as this one is to come to see better how your story is part of the Christian story, how your story contributes to God's saving activity in the world. Throughout this retreat you will be asked to reflect on your relationship with yourself, with others and with God. All three are intertwined, forming one story that grows out of both your graced story (your joyful response to God in your life) and your sinful story (where you have failed in your relationship to yourself, others and God). No one episode or pattern in your life reflects all of who you are. You will be invited to visit the different textures of your life through the meditations. Remember, the same story (including your story) can be told a number of ways and from various perspectives. This does not make any of these ways or perspectives less true or not true – it simply means they each bring out different aspects of the truth of your life.

The meditations or sessions in this book have been used over several years to preach retreats to a wide range of individuals: health care workers, teachers, accountants, single mothers, widows and widowers, priests and nuns, retired professionals and others. They would gather for a day, a weekend or a week, and I would present two meditations per day. The rest of the time they would spend in silence reflecting on the scripture passages or questions that accompany the meditation. Daily Eucharist would also be part of the day's rhythm. The meditations have proven helpful for people who are exploring more intentionally the presence of God in their lives and fashioning appropriate responses that will help them live even more fulfilling, happy and meaningful lives as people of faith. I am confident that the meditations will support you along that same journey.

Note that three additional meditations are available online for purchasers of this book: read or download them at en.novalis.ca/20-Minute-Retreat-Extra-Sessions/. See page 157 for the themes of these meditations.

The Sequence and Themes of the Meditations

Each meditation has a different theme and will take you on a personal journey related to that theme. However, in another meditation, some of the same ideas may arise or be expressed in other ways. This is the nature of being on a retreat: the same idea (or a similar one) may strike you in a new way as you go along. You may find yourself turning over certain ideas so you can look at them in a fresh way and highlight significant aspects of the Christian journey. Even within the same meditation, some ideas may be repeated. You might think, "That's been said already – I know that!" but "knowing that" is not our goal. It's about engaging: just as a retreat master will return to key points several times to allow the meditation to sink in, so do the meditations in this book. You may stand in the same place in a river at various times, but it is not the same water that washes over your feet. Keep this in mind as you read through the meditations.

This book is not about learning abstract ideas: it aims to engage you in your life, your desires for your life, wherever you are at this point in your journey. Yes, you will learn about some historical events, theological ideas and spiritualities; you will be exposed to biblical texts in ways you may not have thought of before, encounter significant Christian authors and their works, or be invited to rethink some previously held convictions. Ultimately, though, the retreat is not about learning anything new unless it helps you reflect on your personal faith story.

Each meditation is meant to stand alone. After you do the first three meditations, called the "Foundations," you could continue your retreat anywhere in the book. Even if there is a passing reference to other content in the book, you do not have to read the other meditation to enter fully into what is being presented. Still, the sequence does follow a certain pathway to help you gradually enter your own story, deepen that journey and gain insight into your desires for your relationship to God. But don't forget, this is also a journey in your relationship with yourself and with others. Although God calls us individually, we always journey as a community called by God to be in solidarity with each other.

That means you are not alone on this retreat. Each meditation includes a "companion."[1] These are saints you may invite to accompany you. Brief biographical notes are given for each saint. Take a few moments before you begin the meditation to pray to the saint and ask him or her to be with you and guide you. You are in good company with these holy companions who will walk with you throughout your retreat.

What is a Saint?

You may think of a saint as somebody who does extraordinary things, works miracles and has lived a life you could never dream of living. But this attitude toward saints does not stand up against the historical witness of the many men and women who lived ordinary lives, like you and me, and came to be known as saints. Saints are better understood not as "miracle workers" but as "models." We are invited to imitate the virtues they lived in their lives as we tread our own pathway with God and to God.

Saints are people who have, over a lifetime, lived virtuous lives of faith, hope and charity. The Church has recognized them as such and invites us to see their lives as models for our own, each one modelling something different. They have lived in a vast range of situations, times and places, just as we too live in a different situation, time and place from them. But that does not stop us from striving to imitate the virtuous life for which they are now recognized.

Saints, therefore, help us understand that Christian holiness is achievable in the concrete circumstances of life: my life, your life. Many improbable men and women have been recognized as saints over the millennia of Christianity, people we may have thought should never have made it. Yet here we are on the same path. Saints give us hope that the life to which Jesus calls us is indeed possible, whatever the circumstances in which we find ourselves, so that we too, in the fullness of God's time, may join their company.

What is a Doctor of the Church?

Some of the companion saints to the meditations are recognized as "Doctors of the Church." Doctors of the Church have been formally identified by the Catholic Church only since the eighteenth century. It takes three things for somebody to be recognized as a "doctor."

First, the individual has something original, meaningful and thoughtful to teach, something that has had an important influence on the life of the Church and its members. Doctors normally have left behind a collection of writings that attest to this characteristic. Second, the individual is recognized as being very holy. Typically, Doctors of the Church are chosen from those already recognized as saints as described above. Third, the Pope needs to issue a formal proclamation indicating the above two criteria have been met.

Thus, Doctors of the Church are recognized as authentic and enduring witnesses to God's love for us. The example of their lives and teachings is worthy of our attention. Regardless of the time in which we live, we have something important to learn from them.

How to Go on Retreat

So how do you go about being on retreat? Below are some suggestions to help frame your retreat. Modify these as needed to meet your personal needs or preferences.

1. **Choose a space**
   › Find a location that is quiet and away from potential distractions (a room with a door you can close, if possible). If other people are around, let them know you will not be available for the next twenty minutes or so. Ask them to respect this time as sacred (which it is) and let them know you will attend to any pressing matters after you are finished.
   › Sit in a comfortable chair.
   › Be sure the lighting is appropriate for reading; have a pen and paper or a notebook handy in case you would like to write down your thoughts or feelings.

> Leave your cellphone in another room. Silence other phones or devices and turn off the TV or radio.

2. **Get started**

> Pay attention to your mood from the beginning. Check in with yourself: How are you feeling? What are you thinking about? Are you having any physical discomfort? Acknowledge these and try to put them aside temporarily to focus on the meditation. Also set aside any major events from the day – stressful encounters, pressing problems, unresolved challenges.

> Begin with a brief prayer. First, invite the companion of the meditation to be with you. After reading the brief biography, pray to the saint and ask him or her to be with you over the next twenty minutes or so. Second, pray a short prayer to God, who is also with you in the meditation. You could use words like these:

> *Loving God, I come before you in these moments of silence to open my heart to you. Bless this silence with the presence of your Holy Spirit. May I be open to listening to you and following you ever more deeply in my life in all ways. Thank you for this time together. Amen.*

> Read through the meditation slowly. Pause as needed to reflect. Reread it, if you like.

> Work your way through the reflection questions. Take your time. Jot down some thoughts or feelings as you reflect.

> End with a brief prayer of thanksgiving, such as *Gracious God and Saint [name], I am grateful for this time together. Thank you for your presence in*

my life. Be with me until we come together in retreat once again. Amen.

3. Keep a journal

> Consider keeping a journal (notebook) in which you can jot down thoughts or feelings or brief summaries of events from your life that seemed meaningful during the meditation or as you reflect on the questions at the end.

> Keep this journal in a private and safe place for your personal use. You can destroy it after the retreat if you feel it contains too much personal information and you don't want others to read it.

Putting Together a Longer Retreat

Create a schedule for your retreat. There are twenty-one meditations (eighteen in this book and three online): use them at your own pace. Below are some rhythms you can try. Once you have chosen your rhythm, stick to it as best you can. Deciding to do the next meditation whenever you have time risks losing your focus as well as the dynamics of listening to your inner self and listening to God. These dynamics are nurtured through staying with the meditations over a defined period. Perseverance will reward you. Note: Each option begins with the Foundations (Meditation One: Where Do I Encounter God?; Meditation Two: Telling Your Story of Faith; and Meditation Three: Cast Your Net into the Sea: Setting out on the Journey). The sequence of these three foundational meditations moves you first to a focus on God in creation, next to your story in God and God's creation, and finally to your own current desires, which you bring before God during this retreat. Each option also finishes with Meditation Eighteen: The Journey Travelled: The Quest to Live Symbolically. This final meditation ties together whichever rhythm you have followed during your retreat.

> **One-week retreat:** Foundations plus three other meditations of your choice; finish with Meditation Eighteen. Once you have finished the Foundations on the first three days of your retreat (back to back), schedule the other meditations over the next four days – one per day – according to which themes interest you and what is relevant at this time in your life. By the end, you will have completed a one-week retreat. This pattern could be repeated as time allows until you have finished all the meditations.

> **Two-week retreat I:** Foundations plus seven other meditations of your choice; finish with Meditation Eighteen. Once you have finished the Foundations on the first three days of your retreat (back to back), schedule over the remainder of the two weeks eight time periods (one per day) when you know you will be available. Put these in your calendar and avoid rescheduling them if you can. Select seven meditations based on your interests and what is relevant at this time in your life; finish with Meditation Eighteen. By the end, you will have done a two-week retreat. You can repeat this rhythm with the rest of the meditations as time allows. Note: This option allows you to not schedule a few days when you know you will be unable to fit time into your schedule.

> **Two-week retreat II:** Foundations plus two meditations per day in sequence until you have completed them

all; finish with Meditation Eighteen. The first day and half of your retreat are the Foundations: one in the morning and one in the afternoon (or the evening, if that suits your rhythm better). Over the following two weeks or so, continue the meditations in the order provided: one in the morning and one in the afternoon or evening, finishing with Meditation Eighteen. Follow this option when you know you will be available to do a twenty-minute meditation twice a day over a fourteen-day period. Put these times in your calendar and avoid rescheduling them if you can. By the end, you will have done a two-week retreat.

> **Four-week retreat:** Foundations plus one meditation per day in sequence until all meditations are complete, finishing with Meditation Eighteen. Once you have finished the Foundations on the first three days of your retreat (back to back), schedule over the following four weeks the remaining eighteen meditations (one per day) on days that you know you will be available to do the twenty-minute meditation. Put these in your calendar and avoid rescheduling them if you can. By the end, you will have done a four-week retreat. Note: This retreat takes place over four weeks, taking account of the fact that there may be five or six days when you may not be able to schedule your twenty-minute meditation. Ideally, you would schedule one per day over twenty-one days in sequence.

Being on Retreat with Others

You might consider inviting a trusted friend or two to do the retreat with you. I would not recommend more than two others, for the practical reason of scheduling and the dynamics of building a trust relationship over the course of the retreat.

> You will need to decide which option to follow from those listed above. Each of you will do the same meditations each day, even though the time of day might differ slightly depending on your schedules. You will need to keep the same pace throughout the retreat.

> Plan on having a conversation of fifteen to twenty minutes each day during the retreat after you have completed the meditation(s). The focus of the conversation would be the Questions for Prayerful Reflection or any other insights that came to you during the meditation. This is where keeping a few notes can be helpful; they will assist you in gathering your thoughts to share. You can have the conversation by phone, if needed. It is easy to set up a three-way call (if two others are involved) on most phones.

> You will still do the retreat alone, in that each participant has their own prayer space, reads the meditation alone and takes time to reflect on the questions on their own.

Even if you do the retreat on your own, you are never fully alone; you are with the companion saint for each meditation. Ask these saints to accompany you all the way and they surely will. You are also in communion with all men and women who seek a deeper and more meaningful relationship with God, *the desire* for our lives. Pray for them while you do your meditations; knowing that they are also praying for you will help you feel supported.

May God bless you as you move into your sacred journey in these days of retreat.

Remember to download the three additional meditations that are available online:
en.novalis.ca/20-Minute-Retreat-Extra-Sessions/

Foundations

Meditation One
Where Do I Encounter God?

Companion of the Meditation: Patron Saint of Missionaries: Teresa of Kolkata (1910–1997)

Teresa of Kolkata was the youngest of three children born to Nikila and Drane Bojaxhiu in the city of Skopje, part of Serbia at the time. Baptized as Agnes, she had a family nickname, Gonsha. The family was financially comfortable, and she knew no shortage in her childhood, but her father died when Agnes was eight, which considerably reduced the household income. At eighteen she joined the missionary Institute of the Blessed Virgin Mary (commonly known as the Loreto or Loretto Sisters) and took the religious name Mary Teresa, after Thérèse of Lisieux. In this community all the sisters are called by their second name and, so she became Sister Teresa. In 1929 she travelled to Kolkata, India, as a missionary and taught for twenty years. Eventually she experienced a call from God to dedicate her life to the poor; it was there, in the poor, that she encountered God. To pursue this calling from God, she left the Loreto Sisters and established a new religious congregation called the Missionaries of

Charity. This order has since spread throughout the world, always seeking out and ministering to the "poorest of the poor." Today, Sister Teresa of Kolkata is known all over the world as Saint Mother Teresa.

For the person of faith, every human experience, in whatever setting, has the potential to break open the reality of God.[2] Every human experience has the potential to reveal the "ultimate mystery," which is God. God speaks to us in all the places where we hang our hat. If we have ears to listen, the simplest gesture of another human being, a brilliant sunset, a quiet morning stroll, dropping a glass on a hard surface and having it smash to bits, the busy noise of a highway, recovery following an accident – all these experiences and more can summon us to another level in our relationship with God. The distinction between what is holy and what is not is a question of awareness and discernment, rather than a predetermined decision about what these things represent in themselves.

Christian faith always blossoms in a context: a location (including geography and climate), historical setting (including current political affairs, economic realities and social elements), and culture (including nuances of language, ethnic background and values). These factors influence and shape the dynamics of Christian faith in the life of the believer. This is the spirituality of time and place.

We may think a spirituality is best explored through studying the writings of its significant figures, prayer practices, rituals and so on. But geography, climate, culture, politics, social location (such as whether we are better off financially or poorer; a politician or a skilled labourer), ethnic background and other factors also play a role. Because we are embodied in one place, we need to understand the richness of time and place in our development as Christians. We encounter this truth in the life of Mother Teresa of Kolkata, in her encounter with the poor. She blossomed in the streets of Kolkata, where she met the poor in all their life challenges. And she is saying the same thing to us: meet God's people wherever you are:

> And so here I am talking with you. I want you to find the poor here, right in your own home first. And begin love there. Be that good news to your own people first. And find out about your next-door neighbours. Do you know who they are?[3]

Another example is Francis of Assisi (c.1181–1226), who also was influenced by his context. His spirituality did not emerge through withdrawing from or avoiding the social and political issues facing him; rather, it emerged because he embraced and responded to these issues. We see this in the clear choices he made in his life – choices that were based on his Christian faith, how he understood and was in relationship with God. Francis felt a great solidarity with the poor, like Teresa of Kolkata; he began to share whatever he had, and spent a great deal of time in their company.

But Francis' new lifestyle clashed with his family's expectations. As a cloth merchant, his father exploited the poor by underpaying them, and the working conditions in the factory were atrocious. The empathetic Francis sided with the workers. His father tried to dissuade him from solidarity with the poor and the socially outcast, to the point of locking him up in the house. But Francis was not deterred. He remained with the poor and gave up his family inheritance to pursue his dream.

These brief stories of the lives of Francis of Assisi and Teresa of Kolkata, the companion saint with you in this meditation, show how our Christian lives have social and political references. Context drew them into a new life of faith in a practical way. But beyond these practical circumstances of life that are dictated by place, the imaginative dimension of human living and the construction of personal identity are also engaged by the geography where we live.

A particular geographic location, such as the desert, may allow for the development of a symbol system and personal identity that are markedly different from that of another geographic location, such as a forested mountain. In the desert, water is scarce. There, our dependence on water for survival will be a constant in our lives. In the forested mountains, meanwhile, water is likely plentiful. When we take for granted that it is present in the forested mountain, we may appreciate water more for its aesthetic value as it tumbles down the quaint waterfalls and bubbling brooks. But the reflection on water in these two situations may evoke different images and feelings, as well as engaging different life experiences. How a person identifies meaningfully with water, therefore, may vary depending on where they live. Water is an important Christian symbol. Thus, how the symbol of water or water itself has the potential to break open God's presence in one's world will be influenced by the geographical setting.

The above statements are no less true for the city, even though we construct our city landscapes (perhaps best called *cityscapes*) in ways that are radically different from those of the desert. In the desert we find ourselves largely powerless before the forces of nature, whether benevolent or hostile. Cities, on the other hand, are more directly tied to the imaginative human creations of architecture, the planning of transportation systems, parks, marketplaces, residential and business areas, and so on. A critical reflection on the impact of cities on the development of our Christian faith and community life is of the utmost importance, since so many people today live in cities.

City space and its accessibility directly affect human interaction and influence our access to each other and to our humanity. This is also true for public places of business and commerce. We see how small towns, with their markets for fresh food, cafés for unhurried conversations, and places of worship, all clustered in one area, continue to provide a meaningful place for human encounter. Larger cities may be challenged to provide this setting.

We see that the symbols and images we incorporate into our faith life are all drawn from the real-life experiences shaped by our surroundings. The stories we tell about our lives that reflect our faith are influenced by the context in which we live. In short, the impact of context (time and place), described as the meaningful place in which we live, act, love, enjoy the company of others and so on, is an essential category of human experience that shapes identity and our Christian faith at both the personal and community levels.

Regrettably, the world suffers from the historical expulsion of any sense of the divine from the physical world and from the everyday milieu of human encounter. We are not used to talking about God being present with us in the everyday of life; we find it difficult to feel that God is with us. We ask, "Where is God in my life?" It's not difficult, at least from one perspective, to understand why we often find ourselves asking this question.

Following the rapid increase of the development of the different sciences in the seventeenth century, scholars and the population at large began to look at the world as a mere object to be studied and used for human advancement. Everything has a knowable cause; we just have to discover it. Science began to unlock the mysteries of the universe and human living. This led to the tendency to describe the world in terms of cause and effect, as if we were describing the working parts of a giant clock with its cogs and wheels. The mysterious nature of the universe tended to get lost, and the mystery of God was similarly relegated to the sidelines. God was not to be found in our world or in our life experience, but was far away – in heaven somewhere.

Increasingly, the Divine's personal encounter with humanity was dismissed to the privacy of one's interior feelings or, conversely, limited to when one went to church. The former risked putting a priority on popular piety over public worship, while the latter tended to assume that ritual performed in restricted "holy" places was the only way to encounter the Divine in the world.

With the generalized expulsion of the Divine from the world, many faith-based communities felt little need to give attention to social action (that is, denouncing injustices, such as slavery and apartheid), address equality issues between men and women or between societies as unique groups, or raise ecological issues in the public forum (the destruction of rain forests or the pollution of water and air). This needed to change.

But we resist change. Adults brought up in one framework find it difficult to live out of another. Thus we need to continually and consciously be attentive to how God is present in all we do.

We must strive to avoid a privatized faith that sees "the world out there" as having little or nothing to do with our faith life.

Slowly, Christians have realized the harm done by the failure to recognize that *the world* is God's dwelling place. God can be encountered in churches and in the countryside, in mosques and on mountaintops, in temples and among trees. God can be encountered in the face of the poor, the prisoner, the outcast, in the struggles of everyday life, in blessings and joys shared with family and friends, in moments of transition such as weddings and retirements, funerals and tragedy. In short, all experience can reveal that God is with us if we take the time to listen. Both Teresa of Kolkata and Francis of Assisi realized this and followed their hearts to respond to God's call in their lives.

A desire to locate ourselves meaningfully in the world in relationship with this sacred dimension has given birth to new ways of living our Christian faith. Perhaps you desire to live more fully in the sacred dimension. How do you decide what is helpful and what is not to develop your faith life? Should you belong to an organized faith community or go to church on a regular basis? Is it enough to go to church occasionally (Christmas and Easter) and not every week? Your answer to these questions is important, and is worth pondering. The world today hungers for authentic meaning: you are on that same quest. Living Christian faith needs to nourish our being at all levels. It needs to bring together our head and our heart, so we experience our body-selves as complete and whole (holy).

All these factors and many others are important to recognize as integral to developing one's faith life alongside the traditional Christian resources, such as the stories, poems and psalms in the Bible, the teachings of the Church, and biographies of holy men and women. Against this backdrop, your own story takes shape. Your experiences are integral to shaping and telling your own story and how you fit into the larger Christian story.

....

Questions for Prayerful Reflection

1. Describe the physical place where you live. Do you consider it a holy place? Why or why not? If not, what prevents it from being a place where God dwells and where you can meet God?

2. How do you experience being immersed in a world that separates the sacred from the everyday? What small step could you take to connect more closely what you feel in your soul, know in your head and believe through the eyes of faith?

3. Do you think your surroundings, for example, geography, climate and buildings, can be a place in which God's presence is mediated to you? Why or why not?

4. Do you sometimes feel that you are a cog in a giant machine? If so, take a moment to appreciate that God does not see you that way. Ask for God's grace so you will not feel that way about yourself, either.

5. Where do you go for spiritual nourishment? Is it integrated into your life or separate from it? How could you bring the two together? If you belong to a church community, what expectations do you have about the relationship between this community and your daily life?

Meditation Two
Telling Your Story of Faith

Companion of the Meditation: Patron Saint of Authors: Francis de Sales (1567–1622), Doctor of the Church

Born in Savoy, France, Francis had a troubled childhood due to ill health. Gradually he grew stronger and vowed to dedicate his life to God. He loved books and was eager to learn; at the Collège de Clermont in Paris, he studied under the Jesuits. Eventually, Francis was ordained a priest and consecrated bishop of the Diocese of Geneva. He constantly searched for ways to reach the hearts and minds of the people during the time of the Protestant Reformation. His writing began with him penning and distributing pamphlets dealing with various questions of Christian life. His sermons were also well received and influential in stirring up the Spirit of God in people's hearts. Two of his well-known books are *Treatise on the Love of God* and *Introduction to the Devout Life*. The latter was written especially for lay people, a highly unusual approach at the time.

True devotion... does not prejudice any calling or employment, but, on the contrary, adorns and beautifies them all. All sorts of precious stones cast into honey become more glittering, each one according to its colour; and all persons become more acceptable in their vocation when they join devotion to it. (*Introduction to the Devout Life*)

The measure of love is to love without measure. (*Treatise on the Love of God*)

Everybody loves a good story.[4] Whether it is told on the big screen, performed as an opera or read from the tattered pages of a favourite childhood storybook, we all enjoy story-telling and story-receiving in differing ways throughout our lives. Stories have that effect on us: they take us to the action, transform us into one of the participants and draw us into the intrigue that seeks to be resolved.

In Christian life, many of our revered texts act upon us in the same ways: they take us to the heart of the action. They transport us into their world so we can be part of the story. This is not to suggest that the Christian stories are fiction. They are not. But all stories, whether fiction or historical, hold much in common. Christian stories – similar to, let's say, novels – play a central role in the development of our lives because they reflect values and outcomes that are important to us. Christian stories allow us to absorb a world of values and action that reflects the long-standing wisdom of the Christian traditions and our relationship with God.

Francis de Sales, your companion in this meditation, knew this well. He was constantly writing about the value of the Christian story through responding to important questions of Christian life that surfaced during his time. He also told stories through his sermons, which stirred up feelings in people's hearts that moved them closer to God. Here we see how important the Bible is in telling the Christian story.

A central role in Christian life is the biblical witness of men and women and their stories of life with God, with each other and within the cosmos. The Bible is a primary text for the development of Christian life, moral development and character. In fact, we could describe the scriptural witness to the saving activity of God in our lives as *the* most important text. It holds special prominence in the life of Christian communities and individuals within them. Thus, you will be invited to reflect on a good number of biblical stories throughout your retreat. However, many kinds of other texts are also of great significance in Christian life and are used to foster insight, growth and maturation.

These include the many biographies and autobiographies of the lives of Christians who have gone before us. Christian prayer books, hymnals, sermons, letters and poetry are also important. But what about Christian musical scores, religious icons, statues, paintings, architecture and other works of art that express Christian life and nourish the soul? Can these also be read as "stories"? Yes, they can. For example, the musical scores and paintings of the German mystic Hildegard of Bingen (1098–1179), who gave witness to her visions from God through these media, are valuable resources for faith development. Indeed, all these expressions that stem from Christian life could be "read" as stories. They, too, take us up into the action of faith life expressed in these media. Each, in its own way, captures and portrays the faith experience of the artist who sculpted, painted, wove tapestries, wrote icons and so on.

You, too, have a story. You have a past and a present, and you have desires for your future. Each meditation in this book will help you explore your story, engage it at various levels and deepen your understanding of it through the eyes of faith. You will be invited to view past and current memories, or perhaps even painful memories that you may have long ago discarded. We can always learn more from our experiences, from our stories, especially when we view them through the eyes of faith. Doing so can help us appreciate them in a fresh new way, perhaps in a way that has never occurred to us before. Thus, attentiveness is important when you tell your story and insert yourself into the stories of others told through these meditations. You will discover new things about yourself.

Perhaps you are an artist and tell your story in artistic form. For example, the expression on the face of a statue (sad, longing, joyful, hopeful), gestures of the hands (outstretched, arms folded, pointing, wringing, clasped), even colours (dark, light, monochromatic, mixed) speak to realities beyond the concrete existence of the work of art itself. Through these "gestures," a story is told; we are drawn into levels of reflection beyond the statue before us. We are led to interpret our own lives through these variables of the statue: What does the statue "say" to us?

Note that feelings are part of reading the story told by the artistic production. Through those feelings, we gain meaning from the piece of art. That's why it is important to be aware of your feelings as you ponder each meditation and reflect on the prayerful questions at the end. Feelings reveal what is going on in our lives; if we ignore them, we may miss out on how God is speaking to us at a deeper level. Beyond the head (knowing) lies the heart (feeling); both are needed for self-discovery and exploring how your story fits into the larger drama of the Christian story.

Meaning from our faith life can be expressed and preserved through these art forms, and we can recognize our own journey through them. They take up and voice the truthfulness of the way God has been in relationship with God's people. Let us briefly look at an example from the world of artistic expression: that of Hildegard of Bingen, mentioned above.

In Hildegard's paintings, we see a struggle to break free of accepted patterns of oppression (feudal master over common labourer; man over woman; cleric over layperson). Her cosmic vision of inclusivity and equality of all people, as expressed in her art, witness to this dimension of God's saving plan for the world. Hildegard's expression of the sanctity of all life is another powerful dimension of her artistic work. She recognized a deep relationship among the love of God, the love of the natural world and artistic expression.

With Hildegard, the expression of life's beauty through art can bring us into relationship with God and with one another in ways that cannot be anticipated. Art that moves us to rejoice and be happy – or to cry and be mournful – directs our emotions toward the transcendent nature of life, just as written stories do. Art produces worlds in which our imaginations can wander. This opens new possibilities for our lives and helps us to grow the values and virtues we desire.

The example of Hildegard of Bingen challenges you to be open to the ways God's love is lived and celebrated in your life and can move you to grow and mature. You may not have experienced visions like Hildegard of Bingen, but the presence of God's Spirit in your life is just as real. You need to believe you are part of the dynamic Christian stories being passed along for others.

These stories use figures of speech, parables, poetry and other imaginative literary devices to convey meanings and truths about life, about ourselves (our character) and about God, although these truths are not immediately available to us. It is because stories are highly charged and open to multiple meanings that we need to take time to reflect upon them.

Another example of how stories bring great depth of meaning to life are the fourteenth-century writings of Julian of Norwich (1342–1414). In her *Revelations of Love*, Julian recounts her painful love affair with Christ. Her religious experience was shaped by the enormous loss of human life due to the bubonic plague (Black Death) that spread across Europe at that time. What does this story mean? The story contains the author's intended meaning, but this may not be the only or final meaning. We could stop at saying that Julian's visions represent an imaginative attempt to meaningfully express the absurdity of death that surrounded her in the small English town of Norwich and throughout Europe. But how does this acknowledgement help you understand your experience of death and pain today when *you* have a tumultuous experience? We need to go beyond merely acknowledging the origins and truths of the story related to its time of production. This is how we write our own story: by reading the stories of others to better understand our own experiences.

This approach acknowledges the importance of your experiences, which gives the text new life. Francis de Sales says faith "does not prejudice any calling or employment." You are involved in a life-world – a world of family life, work, prayer, self-giving, faith community and so on, which is important. What do these meditations mean for you today, given that your life-world is likely quite different from the life-world during which the text was written? The cumulative experience of your life, your history of relationships and the current situations in which you find yourself are all brought to bear on your prayerful reading of these meditations.

When you approach them in this way, the meditations are kept supple and fluid, and you leave room for the dynamic nature of your life and the active presence of God to enter your life. In this way these meditations can contribute significantly to your personal spiritual-human maturation. When you remain open to new ways that God speaks to you to renew your life in a changing world, you can develop a deeper sense of how the Christian story is alive in your life. Throughout this book you will be continually invited to "write" your own story by reflecting on it in fresh ways through the lens of Christian faith.

Biblical stories, the central Christian text, always invite you to reflect on your own life in a similar way to the examples given above. While reading the biblical stories, you are invited to insert yourself into the drama whether, for example, it is Jesus addressing his disciples or Paul instructing the communities he has visited to live better moral lives.

The Bible stories were written by people who believe, suffer, hope, forgive, love and find joy in life. So we ask: How does the story speak to my/our current world, where all of my believing, loving and forgiving take place? What new possibilities does the story open up as it shapes anew my ideas about God, myself and the world in which I live?

At first, you may feel your story is not interesting or that you don't have a lot of significant events or experiences to reflect upon. Or perhaps you feel the opposite – that so much has happened in your life, you don't know where to begin to pick out what is important. Neither of these situations is what is being addressed in these meditations. Your story is the place where God is speaking to you – in whatever circumstances you now find yourself. The task is to take the time, with these meditations, to be in touch with how this is true, so that you experience the mystery of God in your everyday living and grow in a deepening sense of blessing and hope for your life and the lives of others. This is God's desire for you.

You are a storyteller, and your story is worth telling because God is at the origin of it.

Questions for Prayerful Reflection

1. Have you ever considered your life story as part of the bigger Christian story and part of the story of the Christian men and women who have gone before you? Think of one event in your life that is like something you have read or heard in the Bible. Ponder this for a few minutes.

2. What role do your feelings play in your faith journey? Do you believe God can speak to us through our feelings, as explained in this meditation? Place yourself back into a recent situation where you felt happy, or sad, or angry, or peaceful, or despairing, or alone, or joyful (or a mixture of these). Ask God to help you be aware of how the way you felt was part of how God was speaking to you.

3. What would it mean for you to write your own story, as countless men and women have done over the history of Christianity? This does not mean to write your history from the beginning to the current moment. It means writing down occasional meaningful events that you experienced as being of God or inspired by God, as you recall these events through the eyes of faith. You are invited to do exactly this during this retreat. Keep a journal in which you can jot down thoughts, or feelings, or brief summaries of events that seem meaningful to you when reflecting on the questions at the end of each meditation. You could start by writing down something about the above two questions.

Meditation Three

Cast Your Net into the Sea: Setting Out on the Journey

··

Companion of the Meditation: Patron Saint of Fishers: Peter (1– c. 64), Apostle

Peter was born in the region of Galilee in the town of Bethsaida. Peter was married, caught fish for a living and lived an ordinary fisherman's life until his dramatic encounter with Jesus in Galilee. He was originally called Simon, but Jesus, upon meeting him, called him Peter ("rock"): it was upon this rock Jesus intended to build his Church, as he announced that day. Peter's dedication to Jesus was obvious, but so too was his ambiguous response at times to Jesus' call to come follow him with full commitment. For example, Peter denied knowing Jesus when public opinion turned against Jesus. Eventually, Peter gave his life entirely over to continuing Jesus' ministry after Jesus died and rose, but had a personal journey of conversion to make in taking up his own cross and following Jesus. He met a violent and painful death at the hands of the Roman authorities while on a missionary trip to Rome in the mid-60s. He is recognized as the first Pope.

Jesus said to them, "Children, you have no fish, have you?" They answered him, "No." He said to them, "Cast the net to the right side of the boat, and you will find some." So they cast it, and now they were not able to haul it in because there were so many fish. That disciple whom Jesus loved said to Peter, "It is the Lord!" When Simon Peter heard that it was the Lord, he put on some clothes, for he was naked, and jumped into the sea. (John 21.5-7)

We begin with a story about Jesus walking along the seashore. We can imagine it was earlier in the day. The people in the boat had been working hard. Peter worked so hard that he removed his outer garment, as the heat of the day was beginning to build. The crew had been out since early morning. They were tired and felt down because of their lack of success in fishing.

As Jesus walked along, he called out to these strangers as "friends." He saw their need and counselled them to keep trying. Do we really believe that they had not yet tried, with their experience as fishermen, the spot on the right side of the boat where they eventually found their catch? What was different this time? Something new – rather, *someone* new – entered the events of the moment. Jesus' presence transformed everything for Peter and the other fishermen.

In this encounter with Jesus, nothing became an abundance. The emptiness was filled. The need of the fishermen to feed their families, sustain life and return home successful had been satisfied. Life could continue with confidence following the encounter with Jesus.

Such is the pilgrimage on which we embark with this meditation. We get into a boat together and go fishing and we bring our pilgrim heart with us. Wonder, hope and intrigue accompany us. Along with Peter and his friends, we cast our nets. Will Jesus come along and call us "friends"? Will he fill our need? Quench our thirst? Provide a moment of insight into our lives? In short, will he fill our nets with whatever we need at this point in our lives?

What we note in the story about the fishermen is that the first moment of encounter with Jesus was a moment of trust. From the beginning, Jesus engaged them as people worthy of his friendship. Jesus called out to them as friends, right away, transforming the moment of a stranger meeting strangers into one of a friend meeting friends. From then on, they would meet the challenge of whatever was to follow.

It wasn't only the lack of fish that bothered Peter and the fishermen – it was also the deeper feelings of failure, lack of confidence in themselves and a fear of returning home empty-handed. Jesus engaged these feelings in his simple embrace: "I call you friends." They trusted what he said and cast their nets again. Relationship is all they needed to move forward – the belief that somebody cared. How many times they had cast into that very spot we do not know, but empowered with the friendship now securely in place, they ventured forth again.

Then, their eyes were opened to who this man was. It took an act of trust to move into this deeper level of encounter – to meet this stranger on the shoreline as Jesus the Lord. Letting go of their fear, they cast their nets again in confidence, and their nets were filled with the presence of the Lord. Jesus makes himself fully available to us in friendship today as well. We need only trust that, as we cast our nets, we will also encounter

Jesus waiting for us, ready to call us "friend." Jesus walks along the shore of our lives. Do we have the courage to heed his call, cast our net and venture forth with him?

We begin with a trust that Jesus is with us and that we will encounter him in a new way. We trust that he will fill our nets with what we need and that what little we have will become more than enough.

Jesus seeks to meet us in the ordinary events of our lives. We need to learn this lesson over and over, as did Peter and the others. We need to develop an attentive listening for the footsteps of Jesus. Here, the Holy Spirit sneaks in and whispers in our hearts, "You are my beloved." Jesus never calls out to us without leaving his Spirit of Love. We can never be the same after that. From our empty net comes a new fullness, a new way of encountering others based on this word alive in our hearts: "You are my beloved."

An encounter with Jesus is always transformative. His Word becomes the spirit of our lives – the newness with which we greet others as we walk along the shorelines of their lives. We see Peter and friends in their boat – frail and discouraged – and like Jesus we call out, "Friend!" From this moment on everything changes; the journey continues in mutual trust and friendship.

You have begun this retreat. With the book resting in your arms, you sit in your "boat," wherever that boat is moored. What has drawn you to this moment? What have you brought with you on this journey? Do you know which way the winds are blowing? What pilgrim heart are you bringing forward into this retreat? Be brutally honest in reflecting on these questions. Your answers are neither right nor wrong, just honest. If you are honest, things can change in your life so you become the person you desire to be before God, for yourself and for others.

Does something in your life hold you back from entering fully into this retreat – perhaps certain fears or preoccupations? Take a moment to write them down. Date the page. Return to what you have written as you begin each meditation. Has anything changed? Have you let go of any concerns? Are there new ones to record?

What will allow you to read each meditation in freedom and joy? Take a moment to record these. Date the page. Return to what you wrote at the beginning of each meditation. Has anything changed? Have you celebrated and embraced moments of insight into the way God is alive in your life and whispering in your ear as you encounter Jesus along the shoreline of your life?

We trust that our lives have a purpose in the life of God. But we also know we are a pilgrim people – we are always in a mode of discovery, of deepening our life in God as our small boat journeys along. We need to be in touch with our desires for our life – how we want to encounter God in what is happening today.

What desire do you hold for your life today? For the life of your family? Your friends? How fully in touch are you with these desires? Can you put them into words and write them down? Be as clear and honest as possible, and remember to date the page. From time to time, ask yourself these questions of desire again. Each time, write down your answers. Are they the same as before? If something has shifted or changed, do you know why? Have certain events caused you to change the desires that you hold for your life?

What is being proposed is that you interpret your life in light of the gospel. In interpreting the gospel through the help of the Christian scriptures, authors and artists who have gone before us, Church teachings, liturgical rites and so on, we accept God's saving grace. We need to be our own person with respect to the Christian faith. Although the writings and works of the saints and others are inspiring, nobody can do this work for us. Hildegard of Bingen had this in mind when she wrote the following in her book *Scivias*:

> We cannot live in a world that is not our own, in a world that is interpreted for us by others. An interpreted world is not a home. Part of the terror is to take back our own listening, to use our own voice, to see our own light.[5]

As you progress through your retreat, may you "see your own light." May you be in a better position to understand and embrace how God is calling you closer, how God is "lighting up your life" with and for others.

. . . .

Questions for Prayerful Reflection

1. If you were to name three fundamental values in your life at this time, what would they be? Why is each one important to you now?

2. What do you bring with you on your spiritual journey that you hold most dear (such as time alone, community with others, friendship with particular people)? Do you know why each is important to you and what role each plays in your life?

3. As you sit in reflection with this meditation, what do you need to embrace in your life and what do you need to let go of – at least for a little while – so you can move forward? What are you holding on to "just in case," but would be better off without?

4. As you contemplate the various themes and meditations, are there any distractions that will keep you from casting your net? What are they? What will prevent you from bringing Jesus' freely given generosity and friendship into your boat?

The Journey Continues

Meditation Four

The Ordinary of Our Lives: Birthing Something New

....

Companion of the Meditation: Patron Saint of Pregnant Women and Midwives: Raymund Nonnatus (1204–1240)

The origin of Raymund (or Raymond) Nonnatus' status as patron saint of pregnant women originates in the experience of his own birth. "Nonnatus" or "*non natus*" is Latin for "not born" – he was born by Caesarean section, his mother having died in childbirth before he saw the light of day. Given this experience of coming into the world, he is recognized as the patron saint not only of pregnant women, but also of childbirth, midwives and children. Raymund Nonnatus, a priest, was also known for his strict observance of the confidentiality of confession, which was lax in some circles at the time. As a result, he is also known as the patron saint of priests defending the confidentiality of confession. In Spain and other Latin countries, there is a popular devotion to him where the faithful place a padlock at an altar where he is being revered. The padlock represents prayer requests to end gossip, rumours, false testimony and other sins of the tongue against them. They also represent the sanctity of truthful speech and confidentiality. Raymund Nonnatus did not publish books or write noteworthy sermons. His legacy is honest, truthful speech and a devout life lived so that others could find a new beginning, a new birth.

So that they may know, from the rising of the sun and from the west, that there is no one besides me; I am the Lord, and there is no other. I form light and create darkness, I make weal and create woe; I the Lord do all these things. Shower, O heavens, from above, and let the skies rain down righteousness; let the earth open, that salvation may spring up, and let it cause righteousness to sprout up also; I the Lord have created it. (Isaiah 45:6-8)

We trust that in the ordinary times of our lives, the extraordinary appears through an act of faith. This grounds the potential for something new to be born in us. Once we are open to the possibility of God coming again, meeting us on the shore in whatever state of mind we are in, our world can be created again and again and again. Not in dramatic ways, perhaps, but on a human scale.

This is the choice that every day offers: to believe we are deeply cared for and loved. This may be a disarming prospect – that we can be loved through our sinfulness, our lack of authentic compassion and care for others, and even our lack of love for ourselves. In faith we step forth and cast our net into the deep, trusting that it will come back laden with joy and full of the meaningful things for which we long. Is this not why God came to visit us in the person of Jesus? To bring life, life to the full?

We must dare to believe that even with all our wrongdoing, all our mistakes, all our falling short of the mark, we are deeply and personally cared for by the One who loved us into existence. We are the music in God's heart. God's Spirit, residing deep within us, stirs us constantly and nudges us to believe this is true. Our attentiveness to this creative Spirit will birth new things in our lives, new ways of looking at others, ourselves and the world about us. With Raymund Nonnatus we can be the midwife of our desires for our life by being attentive to God pouring God's heart into ours.

The nature of Love itself is the sole reason for this generous outpouring of God's Spirit. God's love sees beyond all our failures and weaknesses and raises us up to be noble creatures of infinite worth. How wonderful is this reality in our lives! New life, new hope, new joy, all given freely.

This is what is dawning today: the birth of being God's beloved through Jesus in the power of the Holy Spirit. The ordinary becomes the extraordinary through the taking up of human life into the life of God. This is the life of the Trinity. We are being called to more deeply live the way the Trinity lives, acts and calls new life into being. Through the birth of Jesus into our world, God created a community with humankind that is irreversible. In birthing God's self into our world, God gave birth to something new in the lives of every one of us: the presence of God's Spirit that accompanies us always, in our joys and blessings, in our moments of failure and frustration, and even in our moments of sin.

God, speaking to Catherine of Siena in a vision, said it this way: "And so that you might have no excuse for looking not at my affection, I found a way to unite gift and giver: I joined the divine nature with the human.... You cannot look at my gift without looking at me, the Giver."[6]

Here is a scripture passage that testifies to this fundamental truth of the Christian life:

> Creation itself will be set free from its bondage to decay and will obtain the freedom of the glory of the children of God. We know that the whole creation has been groaning in labour pains until now. (Romans 8:21-23)

The Incarnation not only involved God taking on human flesh; in turn, human life has been taken up into the life of God. We became part of God's community in a new way when God became part of ours through the Incarnation. The birth of God in Jesus gave birth to something new and extraordinary in our lives – forever.

How amazing it is that human life, in its fragility, weakness and at times deep tragedy, can also be the vessel of divine joy, profound happiness and intense meaningfulness for God! God's outpouring of the Divine Self in Jesus through the power of the Holy Spirit gives God infinite joy. Your life is the vessel for God's happiness. Can you hear God saying to you, "This is my beloved, in whom I am well pleased"? This is the truth of who we are as human beings: vessels of divine joy and deep satisfaction for God.

It is not often that we are in touch with the ever-present birthing of God in our lives. We are in touch with neither the blessing we are before God nor God's invitation to be a similar blessing to others in our lives, our communities and the wider world. A broken dream dwells within each of us. Our dream for our life may seem distant, impossible to realize. We are weighed down by the at times impossible situations we face, our failure to measure up, and our lack of compassion and care for others. We may know we are made for God's glory, but we seldom know the intensity of the joy, happiness and delight that God takes in us – just as we are.

We need to realize that our dream for our life has already been realized in God's deep care and love for us. We have been taken up into God's life: we need to know that this is the most astonishing dream we could ever have for ourselves. God has made all our dreams come true in birthing new life in the world through the person of Jesus. We cannot outrun God's imagination and dream for us. We may, with Saint Augustine, pray, "Our hearts are restless until we rest in thee, O Lord." But the irony is that we may be looking to rest in God while God is already resting in us.

Even amid our conflicted lives, our painful sinfulness, our arbitrary choices, or the sinfulness of gossip and spreading of false rumours that Raymund Nonnatus spoke of in his homilies, God takes deep pleasure in each of us. Creation twinkles with God-dust – a sparkling glow of God-in-the-world. John of the Cross puts it this way:

> That God, wherever there is room – always showing Godself gladly upon the highways and byways – does not hesitate or consider it of little import to find delight with the children of the earth at a common table in the world.[7]

John of the Cross lived in Spain in the sixteenth century. He travelled long distances on foot when he was a leader in his Carmelite community. He knew that the highways – the main roads connecting major centres of the day – were safe and easily travelled. The byways, as they were known then, were the less-travelled routes that connected more remote villages and towns. It was on the byways that robbers would lie in wait for innocent travellers, attacking them and making off with their possessions or even killing them.

John says God does not hesitate to travel with us on all the roads of our life – those that are well-travelled and safe, as well as those that may lead us astray and cause us harm. God is with us, period. Do we really believe this? Do we take the Incarnation seriously and accept that God has taken us into God's life and journeys with us *in joy* on the highways and byways of our life?

Elsewhere, John of the Cross states that the soul's deep satisfaction is "to see that the individual gives God more than it is worth in itself, the very divine light and divine heat that are given to it."[8] What we reflect back to God is what God has given to us: life in God.

Christian holiness involves not flight from the world but flight into the world. The contemplative life of the mature Christian takes delight in all that the world has to offer. Through the Incarnation we have been awakened to God's deep and abiding presence in this world.

Our life, embraced by God, nurtured by God, guided by God, challenges us to weave a garment along the way. We may never believe that we have the right garment to wear, to be "all dressed up" for God, but we stand humbly before God with the garment of our life that we have woven to this point in the belief that this garment makes us radiate before God.

To suggest that we will only encounter God when we are more spiritually dressed up – when we have it all together – is to miss the point of the Incarnation. God is with us now, helping us to sew our beautiful garment in the ebb and flow of life today. We wear what we have, but we keep going, keep sewing, keep weaving, rejoicing in the garment we now wear, all the while aware that it has yet to be completed. We wear our beautiful garment before God in all the events of our lives.

Our lives are an ongoing mixture of pain, misfortune, disobedience, sinfulness, joy, success, happiness, merrymaking, erotic wonder and frivolity. These threads are joined together to weave our garment. God lives in the embrace of all these moments. We too need to embrace and ponder them. Every event of our lives is worthy of careful consideration and thoughtful critique.

Sometimes the garment we wear may be patchy, or look a little worn, or doesn't seem to fit – but we are called to trust in the potentiality of the now that God has provided. We need to continually set out on a journey of reflection and discovery – to keep casting our net. Let us examine our lives carefully to see how this birth of the Divine occurs in our daily choices, in the people we encounter, and in the joys and blessings as well as the disappointments and frustrations.

Whatever your current condition, whatever shortcomings you may be preoccupied with, move forward in faith. Remember, you are never alone in the journey. God's team is right there with you, helping at every moment. God has taken up residence in our hearts. What can go wrong if that is the case?

. . . .

Questions for Prayerful Reflection

1. Call to mind two or three things you have done in your life for which you believe someone close to you would think less of you if they knew. Perhaps you feel that the person simply would not understand. Thus the secret lives on in your heart, and you are a prisoner to it. Ponder these things for a few moments each.

2. Pick one of the two or three things and act out a dialogue as if you were relating it to God. Tell God that God would think much less of you if only God knew. But, in this case, God does know. How does this make you feel? Can you believe that, even in your sin and shame, you continue to be a vessel of God's deep joy? Can you believe that in your sin God is birthing something new?

3. Still reflecting on the thing you chose in question 2 above, act out a dialogue in your mind with a person close to you who you believe would think less of you if he or she knew. Tell that person about the thing you have kept secret and why they would think less of you or even stop caring for you. Listen to yourself. Does it sound reasonable, based on your relationship with that person? Or is it a question of your inability to love yourself that is at stake?

4. Describe the "garment" you have woven and draped about your body to this point in your life. What is it made of? Are the colours bright or subdued? Is it tattered and worn, or is it like new? What can you do to refresh it?

Meditation Five

Trinitarian Life in Jesus

Companion of the Meditation: Saint Hildegard of Bingen (1098–1179), Doctor of the Church

Hildegard of Bingen was the first of the great German mystics. Her accomplishments are many: among them, poet, prophet, artist, theologian, preacher, composer, pharmaceutical scientist, physician and political moralist with a strong sense of justice. She admonished popes and princes, bishops and lay people alike. Her intense journey of faith began at age eight, when she entered religious life. In her mid-teens, Hildegard took monastic vows as a recluse – a custom that involved enclosure in a cell away from all contact with others. Given her limited opportunity for education, she could barely chant the psalms; she never mastered Latin, the language of writing at the time. Her writings reflect this lack of polish and sophistication, but truth and insight do not depend on clever turns of phrase or the capacity to embellish and titillate. Instead, her theological writings were born "of the earth"; they reflected the reality of a woman intimately in love with God but also in possession of a keen understanding of human life. She wrote about her many visions and spoke openly of them, to the point that her religious superiors speculated that she suffered from severe migraine headaches. In 1148 she established her own monastery. Hildegard had profound insight into the life of the Trinity and wrote often about the Trinity, especially the Holy Spirit, in her work.

> And so these three Persons are in the unity of inseparable substance; but They are not indistinct among themselves. How? He Who begets is the Father; He Who is born is the Son; and He Who in eager freshness proceeds from the Father and the Son, and sanctified the waters by moving over their face in the likeness of an innocent bird, and streamed with ardent heat over the apostles, is the Holy Spirit.[9]

Jesus went on with his disciples to the villages of Caesarea Philippi; and on the way he asked his disciples, "Who do people say that I am?" And they answered him, "John the Baptist; and others, Elijah; and still others, one of the prophets." He asked them, "But who do you say that I am?" (Mark 8:27-29)

People have been thinking about Jesus for a long time. During his lifetime, many thought of him as their political saviour. The Romans had ruled the territory surrounding the Mediterranean for decades before Jesus came along. The Jews longed for freedom from the tyrannical power of Rome. Many in the Jewish community believed Jesus was the one who would set them free from political oppression. They called him "king" or "saviour."

Since Jesus sided with the poor, the outcast and sinners, many began to refer to him as "Messiah" or "Word of God." Because they experienced something very personal in their encounter with him, they began naming Jesus as the God they had come to know through the prophets and kings. Their encounter with him caused many a change of heart, emboldening people to take up the task of proclaiming God's love for all as Jesus did. He promised his disciples that the Spirit of God would accompany them along the way and strengthen them in their task.

Some experiences of those who walked with him on the shores of Galilee have been recorded in the Christian scriptures. Those scriptures have been interpreted in a range of ways to suit changing times, cultural situations, political priorities, ecclesial preferences and the like.

A less enlightened example of this is the Christian acceptance of slavery until the nineteenth century. Slavery went unchallenged in the early Christian communities. Reference to it appears in scripture without comment, revealing that it was accepted as a normal part of the social and political structures of the times. That was to change with the bold stance against slavery that key figures in the Quaker community took in the nineteenth century.

The Quakers were founded without a strict list of beliefs, without formally hired ministers and without church buildings. Their response to Jesus' question "Who do you say that I am?" was expressed in their silent communal prayer and their faith in non-violence as central to the Christian response to the life, death and resurrection of Jesus. This perspective brought them to interpret Jesus' core message – that is, who he was – in a new way. The freedom Jesus preached was to be extended to all persons, regardless of ethnicity, social position or financial means. Jesus, from this perspective, can be called "Freedom" or "Equality."

This message of the freedom and equality of all people may seem obvious to us now, but as a response to the question "Who do you say that I am?" it is a relatively novel interpretation of Jesus' core identity. Our understanding of Jesus continues to develop as we respond to the situations of our own day. New insights come not only with fresh interpretations of scripture; we also draw insights from the world of nature, human psychology, new discoveries about the universe and social analysis to delve more deeply into the mystery of God alive in our world. We also need to draw upon our own personal experiences to name God and respond to the question "Who do you say that I am?"

This is what Hildegard of Bingen did. Even though she could barely write, had trouble singing the psalms and had no position or power, she named who Jesus was for her through whatever means she had available. She learned to write poetry and paint, was intensely interested in plants and medicines, and took on issues of justice in the world. Rather than write documents about Jesus, Hildegard responded to his identity through her life.

Today, around the world, people again have different ways of answering the question of who Jesus or God is for them from within their own social, political, cultural, historical and ecclesial perspectives. From within the issues that confront them, people fashion concrete understandings of Jesus. In this way, each individual or community contributes in an original way to the overall understanding of the mystery of the one God embodied in Jesus. God became one of us and gave us God's strength and wisdom, which reflects God's Spirit in us. As John's Gospel says: "[God] will give you another Advocate to be with you forever. This is the Spirit of truth.... I will not leave you orphaned; I am coming to you.... I [am] in you." (John 14:16-20)

What current world issues affect the way we view Jesus? How might we understand how he is present in our world through these issues? What issues in your own life affect the way you view Jesus? If Jesus is to remain relevant, we must constantly attend to the novel ways that God's Spirit offers insight about him in the human heart. Without a living tradition, of which you are an important part, Christianity risks becoming a happy memory of bygone days.

Jesus, the itinerant preacher from Nazareth, preached inclusivity, forgiveness, freedom and justice for all. What he did defined who he was. There was no distinction between acting and being. To answer the question "Who do you say that I am?" is to reflect on Jesus' activities during his life. In these actions, God is revealed in God's innermost person. The actions of Jesus revealed who God was and continues to be in all times, in all places and for all people.

Who is God? What is God like? How do we get to know the unseen God? All these questions are illuminated by reflecting on Jesus' life, death and resurrection. Jesus, ever faithful to his relationship with God, revealed the inner Spirit of God in all he did by engaging the world in which he lived. His engagement with the world called into question all that was not compatible with his relationship with God.

Just as Jesus was in relationship with God, he called all persons to be in relationship with each other. This included a call to reflect on the nature of institutions and their laws. These institutions also needed to reflect the love that God and Jesus shared. God's embodied love, according to Jesus, was not just to take root in the heart of individuals or among persons who cared deeply about each other, but also between people and the institutions that govern, direct and organize their lives.

Jesus' invitation to live life fully extends this opportunity to all. When we fail to reach this goal on a personal level, we can talk about personal sin – we've missed the mark that Jesus set. When an institution or society fails to attain this goal, we talk about social sin. Social sin is revealed in the practices, policies, structures and norms of institutions, communities and groups that do things and engage people in ways that do not allow or encourage Jesus' message of empowering love to take hold. Of course, institutions, communities and groups do not exist in the abstract. They are made up of people like you and me.

Thus the call to conversion of individuals may in turn be leaven for the conversion of oppressive social structures and practices. These speak as witnesses or counter-witnesses as loudly as do the actions and sayings of individuals.

All systems of faith, all beliefs and all practices point to the above truths in some way, even if partially. Religion ought to achieve in us, at least to a certain degree, a "divestment of religion." It is not religion that we seek, but the living God, who cannot be bound even by the most insightful beliefs, practices and institutional norms. We must walk "the way" of Christ through systems that have been built up over the millennia of Christian life. But we must not stop there. We need to keep going beyond the success and the failure of these devices to make present the fullness of our God. Systems may impede as much as they enable us – they are not God and must be transcended. Only God can bring the fullness of God's life, in God's time, in God's ways. The goal is not to prepare for eternal life through appropriate beliefs and practices, but *to live* the next life in this one. We are to live the fullness of the resurrection of Jesus in the here and now by naming who Jesus is for us personally as well as how he can respond to the changing needs of our times.

We are created in the image and likeness of God, a God who is One but Three. This is who God is for us. Hildegard of Bingen reflected on this mystery in many ways. Here is one text where she uses the image of fire to respond to the question of God as Trinity:

> As the flame of a fire has three qualities, so there is one God in three Persons. How? A flame is made up of brilliant light and red power and fiery heat. It has brilliant light that it may shine, and red power that it may endure, and fiery heat that it may burn.[10]

As we name Jesus in our lives, we are naming the presence of the Trinity. Through our life in the Trinity, we too may shine with faith, be a power for change and conversion, and warm the hearts of others so they too may discover this.

· ·

Questions for Prayerful Reflection

1. What visual image of Jesus most readily comes to mind when you pause for a moment? Do you have a sense of where or how this image emerged in your consciousness (such as through school experiences, family devotions, scriptural texts or popular culture)? Describe this visual image of Jesus in words.

2. Who do you say Jesus is for you? Name two or three words that capture who Jesus is for you as you live your daily life.

3. What issues in the world today impact the way you view Jesus? How might you understand the way he is present in our world differently through these issues?

4. With Hildegard of Bingen, do you have a sense that God is three separate persons each present to us in their own way? Can you describe how this is true in your life?

Meditation Six
The Human God-with-Us

Companion of the Meditation: Patron Saint of Headache Sufferers: Teresa of Avila (1515–1582), Doctor of the Church

As reflected in her name, Teresa was born at or near Avila in the Castile region of Spain. When she and her brother Rodrigo were about seven years old, they set out in secret to become martyrs in the country of the Moors. They had not journeyed far when they met an uncle who brought them back to their worried parents. Soon after their return, Rodrigo blamed it all on his younger sister. She later spent a short period of time in a convent, around the age of fifteen, but then returned home. After reading the Letters of Saint Jerome, and acting against the wishes of her father, she secretly went to the convent of the Incarnation of the Carmelite nuns just outside the walls of Avila. Her charity, prudence and personal charm quickly gained her a following and, unusual for the time, she was allowed to receive visitors of all kinds in the parlour of the monastery. However, it was practices like this that led her to launch a reform of the Carmelites, who traditionally had been enclosed in the monastery and largely removed from the external world. She wanted to return to the focus on prayer and contemplation characteristic of monastery life. To assist in this task, she wrote *Way of Perfection* and the book of *Foundations*, along with many others. But her most-read book, *The Interior Castle*, was written for all the faithful. *The Interior Castle* is the basis on which she was named a Doctor of the Church.

The problem is that many folks try to grasp some sense of who I am by taking the best version of themselves, projecting that to the nth degree, factoring in all the goodness they can perceive, which often isn't much, and then call *that* God. And while it may seem like a noble effort, the truth is that it falls pitifully short of who I really am. I'm not merely the best version of you that you can think of. I am far more than that, above and beyond all that you can ask or think.[11]

It may seem strange to start this meditation with a quote from a book of fiction. These words from *The Shack* are useful, however, because they call into question how we envision God and God's presence in our lives. Papa (God) describes Godself as beyond anything we could imagine or think. This is what we refer to as God's "transcendence."

The word "transcendence" conjures up different meanings in people's minds. One's first spontaneous thought on this word may reflect notions of otherworldliness – beyond this world and beyond our capacity to see or understand. But when we think about this carefully, transcendence and the experience of it are not beyond this world. Nor is it beyond our capacity to understand how the dynamics of transcendence are active in our everyday lives.

If we understand "transcendence" as referring to all the intangibles we aspire to, such as peace, joy, happiness and meaningfulness, then we begin to see that it consumes much of our daily preoccupations. Who does not aspire to a purpose in life? Who does not want to participate in something meaningful, thoughtful and creative? Who does not wish to have at least one significant relationship in which we experience being loved, cherished and valued? More than one such relationship would be nice, too. All of these are experiences of human transcendence. They engage the unseen depths of the human soul. They call forth deep emotional investment as well as our time, talent and financial resources.

Think for a moment of how much money is spent around the globe in one month on entertainment and other diversions. Entertainment takes us into worlds of transcendence – worlds of meaning within which we live, if temporarily, through film, music, art – the full range of artistic productions. All of these capture some human aspiration or value – all intangibles, all transcendent, yet remarkably alluring.

The human spirit wades into these moments of transcendence, drinks them up and perhaps becomes open to something new. These moments are formative – they have the potential to shape the human vision from within a different framework. They open us up to new paradigms – new ways of seeing the world and new ways of living our lives. They are not escapist, but they invite us to new possibilities for life. Hope lies in attempting, desiring, wanting to live in these virtual spaces and places, even briefly, allowing us to rest from our burdens that trouble us and can even cripple us.

But what does all of this have to do with Jesus, God-with-us? Think of what Jesus tried to do. Through his life, he asked people to think in a new way about their lives and their faith in God. Jesus asked them to use their imaginations. He told parables to help them envision this new way of being in the world and in relationship with each other and with God.

Parables describe life as possibility: what life could be like for every human person. They engage images drawn from the everyday and use them to invite us to reconsider what we value: intangibles such as peace, love, reconciliation and equality. In short, parables open up the possibility of experiencing transcendence in the here and now.

This is how Jesus explains the purpose of parables in Matthew 13:10-17: they are ways of sharing the secrets of God's life with others. These stories are addressed especially to those who have not experienced God's mysterious life in the world first-hand. In hearing the stories, people are already blessed by God's Spirit, which engages something deep in their souls: "Blessed are your eyes, for they see, and your ears, for they hear." (Matthew 13:16) The miracle of the parables is the transforming effect they have on people's hearts.

Look at the ordinary mustard seed Jesus used to describe the marvels of God's presence in the world – God's kingdom. The mustard seed is an important ingredient in many dishes, but it is tiny. You can barely see it in the palm of your hand. Yet, Jesus uses this speck to describe a wonderful new reality. In Luke 13:18-19, Jesus says, "What is the kingdom of God like? And to what should I compare it? It is like a mustard seed that someone took and sowed in the garden; it grew and became a tree, and the birds of the air made nests in its branches."

Jesus used the mustard seed to describe not his own kingdom, but the Reign of God. From nothing was to come something wonderful that would be the stage for new life. From small beginnings would grow extraordinary new realities. In this kingdom there would be space for new homes, new people, and new ways of experiencing what God values for every person.

Matthew 20:1-16 relates the parable of the labourers in the fields. A landowner hires labourers throughout the day. At the end of the day, all of them receive equal compensation, regardless of when they joined the work crew. Again, we see how Jesus uses an everyday situation to make a point about how God's life with God's people is to be lived. As Jesus and God and the Spirit are equal, so too are all people. Just as all the labourers receive equal pay, no matter how long they worked, God's generous Spirit will be given to those who embrace God's life at any stage of their life. The turning toward God is already the gift of God's life – God's Spirit in their own spirit.

What about God's transcendence? Jesus, God's presence in the world, reveals how close God is to every human person through God's Spirit. In the depth of our hearts, we long for the intimacy shared by God and God's Spirit. This is the spiritual longing that Teresa of Avila wanted to enliven in the hearts of those with whom she was in contact, both within and outside the monastery. Her book *The Interior Castle* aimed to show the many ways God's Spirit is manifest in the human spirit.

The human spirit has an infinite thirst for beauty, for love and for joy – an infinite thirst for transcendence. As noted early in this meditation, we reach for these truths in many ways. But Christians refer to the ultimate accomplishment of these truths as God – the infinite horizon against which all living takes place. This horizon is both so far yet so near in the person of Jesus and the parables he told of God's infinite self-giving love, which bridges the gap between the human and the Divine. What good news this is – the capacity for human beings to experience the fullness of life here and now! But we often forget this truth about our lives.

Teresa of Avila knew how forgetful we can be. But God does not forget and does not leave us alone. She writes:

> For though we know quite well that God is present in all that we do, our nature is such that it makes us lose sight of the fact; but when this favour is granted it can no longer do so, for the Lord, Who is near at hand, awakens it…. The soul experiences a vivid and almost constant love for Him Whom it sees or knows to be at its side.[12]

Given the infinite horizon of meaning toward which humans aspire, human spirit naturally constructs its own parables, its own stories, on how life can be fuller, more just, more generous, more inclusive, more self-giving. This is true whether or not one believes in a personal God. For example, when we make art of any kind, we construct a possible world with transcendent meanings: peace, love, joy, generosity and self-sacrifice. We need not look far in our own world to see how parables of transcendence are being written in the lives of people every day – for example, when we help a stranger, when we welcome a new immigrant and when we share the joy in our heart with others. Like the lowly mustard seed, these need not be earth-shattering, but they do need to be authentic.

A rabbi once questioned one of his cleverer students: "When does night end and day begin?" The student, proud to have the answer at hand, replied, "When we can see the difference between and sheep and a dog." "Good," said the rabbi, "but not correct." The student, a bit deflated but ready to tackle the question again, said, "When we can see the difference between a fig tree and an olive tree from a distance." Again the rabbi responded, "Good. But not correct." The student, stumped, asked, "When?" Quietly, the rabbi said, "When you see a stranger approach, and you see them as a sister and a brother."

When we meet the stranger as a sister or a brother, we meet God. Who do you know that, in small ways, reveals God's face, God's transcendence, in the everyday of life? What parable can you tell of your own life that demonstrates God's nearness in your life and in the communities to which you belong? Getting in touch with answers to these questions reveals how God's ongoing love continues to take root in history and transform your life, other individuals, communities and indeed the world.

. . . .

Questions for Prayerful Reflection

1. What did it mean for you to hear the word "transcendence" before you read the meditation above? Did the meaning of the word shift or change for you? How?

2. People reach for transcendence in various ways, as we saw in the above meditation. How do you do this? What is your story, your parable, of transcendence?

3. How does your desire for and expression of transcendence help you to renew and deepen your faith? What expressions of joy, love, peace, reconciliation, happiness and so on have you experienced?

4. How can you deepen your experiences of transcendence so they become more of who you are?

5. When do you know in a personal way that you reveal God's face – God's transcendence – in the everyday events of your life?

Meditation Seven

Bless One Another as God Has Done

Companion of the Meditation: Patron Saint of Missions: Thérèse of Lisieux (1873–1897), Doctor of the Church

I f anybody can be said to have blessed others as God has done through the ordinary experiences of everyday life, it is Thérèse of Lisieux, popularly known as "The Little Flower." Thérèse's upbringing nurtured her religious perspective. Indeed, all four girls in her family entered the Carmelite order of nuns. The family was comfortable financially – a situation of comfort she eventually rejected to embrace the poverty of religious life. Despite her frailty and illness – a cross she bore throughout her life – she was a beacon of happiness and blessing to all who encountered her. She died of pulmonary tuberculosis at the age of 24. Although she died young and as a cloistered Carmelite nun, her reputation as a kind and self-giving woman spread quickly and widely, beyond her native France – virtually around the world. Her life became known as "the little way" – in the doing of humble things and ordinary daily routines, she exemplified self-giving charity, kindness and love. She blessed everyone who met her. She earnestly wanted to become a priest, but for obvious reasons was not allowed to do so. Instead, she undertook fervent prayer for priests, especially missionaries. The written accounts of her life come largely from her own hand, mostly in her best-selling autobiography, *Story of a Soul*. She also left behind dozens of poems, hundreds of letters and eight plays.

The practice of blessing goes back to the beginning of time. From the earliest days, God blessed the world, the earth and all within it. The Book of Genesis in the Bible speaks of this original blessing, which we could call God's first but abiding blessing: God's steadfast presence in the world through the power of the Spirit given at the time of creation. This is what we read in the Book of Genesis:

> In the beginning when God created the heavens and the earth, the earth was a formless void and darkness covered the face of the deep, while a wind from God swept over the face of the waters. Then God said, "Let there be light"; and there was light. (Genesis 1:1-3)

We know how the story continues. From desolation and chaos came forth the wonderful world that is God's offspring – creation in its entirety. You and I and the world in which we live are all offspring of the bosom of God. As such we are blessed. We came from God's heart, and through God's heart have been given life beyond measure. Then we were profoundly blessed again in the Incarnation – when God became flesh in the person of Jesus. We always need to circle back to these profound blessings in the life given to us and in the Spirit who abides in all of creation. Everything profane is holy in the eyes of God through the original blessings of creation and the Incarnation.

Thérèse of Liseiux lived this reality in earnest. In her writings she stressed that we are all blessed and called to be holy in whatever path we chose and with whomever we find ourselves. Her way of holiness did not imply that we all belong behind monastic walls. Rather, we can bless others through our work, our committed relationships, what we learn from our failures and the routine of everyday living.

Thérèse of Lisieux knew that to have been given life, and to participate in the wonders and joys of this world, is already to be blessed deeply. She continually reminded others of the blessing within which they live. That blessing was given to them freely and needs to be freely passed along to others. To bless another person is to honour the other, to give thanks for their presence in your life and to remind the other that she is born in the image and likeness of God. As such, she is holy (worthy), without further explanation needed. Blessings, therefore, remind us of the closeness of God. God's blessing of closeness can never be taken away.

As baptized members of God's community, we agree to continue passing on the blessings given to us through the way we live with each other. The Christian's role in baptized life is to bless one another as Jesus did. He blessed us by the way he esteemed people in relationships. This is what it means to bless one another and all of creation. Often this blessing is not embodied in something we do, but rather in the way we are with one another. Ultimately, God's blessing is one of presence. To esteem the other is to value the other, to bless the other.

In each breath we take, in the thoughts we think, in the feelings we feel – all of this is subject to the in-breaking of God's baptism, God's blessing, in our lives. We can pass that blessing on to others. Our Baptism challenges us to be convinced of God's care for us, for our brothers and sisters, and for all creation. God is always near. We can enliven this blessing in the way we are present with others and the way we respond to simple situations in everyday life. This is especially important when we feel we have lost our way.

At times we may feel a profound sense of abandonment. We feel alone. God is distant. Perhaps we rarely feel God's closeness. Isaiah had such an experience: "The Lord has forsaken me, the Lord has forgotten me." But God responds: "Can a woman forget her nursing child, or show no compassion for the child of her womb? Even these may forget, yet I will not forget you." (Isaiah 49:14-15)

We have been blessed into an indissoluble community of divine life. Like a mother, God does not forget. Even if a mother does forget, God's promise is beyond the fragility of human ways, and God cannot cease blessing us with loving care. God hovers over us like a mother, constantly present to us. We feel the ebb and flow, the pull and tug, of divine love. We may feel like we are forgotten, but we are not. The original blessing at the time of creation continues through God's abiding blessing of presence in our world and in our hearts.

But what about those closest to us, those with whom we share the deepest parts of our being? Perhaps we feel abandoned by them. We may have stories of how we have experienced neglect or been treated without due consideration. Whether in friendships, married life or partnered life of all kinds, or in significant business relationships, the risk of feeling abandoned or let down is ever present. Ironically, those closest to us can cause the most heartache. Thérèse of Lisieux reminds us that it is not their weakness we should dwell on, but their virtue. That ignoring of others' faults is, for Thérèse, the fullest realization of charity: "I understand now that charity consists in bearing with the faults of others, in not being surprised at their weakness, at being edified by the smallest acts of virtue we see them practice."[13]

When we feel let down, we shouldn't retreat and do nothing. The feeling of abandonment is an opportunity to strengthen the relationship. Just as we would go into silent listening to check out our reality before God, we go to the significant other to discuss what happened. Although we feel vulnerable, we need to bring to light things hidden in the dark. To know is to claim the reality of our existence and to be empowered in moving forward.

In careful consideration, perhaps trusting in a conversation with a dear friend or a spiritual guide, we probe the truth of our lives and relationships, and ponder them before God.

The original blessing in which we participate reminds us that God's work is being accomplished in our lives. God will bring to light in God's time those things that are hidden in darkness. This is baptismal life, the original blessing in which we share. This is Trinitarian life, a life based on trust and hope in God, empowered by the Spirit as Jesus was. With Thérèse of Lisieux we strive to seize any opportunity to bless others. She described her vocation as "not allowing one little sacrifice to escape, not one look, one word, profiting by all the smallest things and doing them through love."[14]

. . . .

Questions for Prayerful Reflection

1. Call to mind two or three areas in your life, or attributes of your person, through which you experience being blessed: places where you receive the goodness of life without earning it. Take a few moments to be present to each of these blessings. Silently give thanks for what you have received and who you are as a person blessed by God.

2. Reflect on the areas of your life or attributes of your person that you called to mind in the first question. Name two or three encounters with others (friends, family members, co-workers, even strangers) where you have blessed them, directly or indirectly. For example: When were you kind to someone even though they upset you? When did you forgive another when, from your perspective, they did not deserve it? When did you give an unsolicited compliment to someone? These are ways we bless others: we recognize their dignity as persons created in God's image and likeness. When these blessings come authentically from your heart, they can radically change the other as well as yourself.

3. Reflect on a time when you felt abandoned, alone, unblessed. What led to this feeling? Recall the experience in the context of the meditation above and reassess. Can you now see the presence of God where you did not before? Can you see blessings emerge? Repeat this exercise with one or two more experiences to see that what you experience in the moment is often not the full reality.

Meditation Eight
Do You Have What You Need?

Companion of the Meditation: Patron Saint of
Embroiderers and Laundry Workers: Clare of Assisi
(1194–1253)

Francis of Assisi came to preach the Lenten mission in Assisi, Italy, when Clare was about eighteen years old. She was so moved by his talks that she sought him out and asked him to assist her in living fully the life of the gospel. She soon sought to join him at his newly established community just outside Assisi. After receiving a simple sackcloth robe and cord from Francis, she was placed in a nearby nuns' convent. Eventually, Francis placed Clare in a poorhouse by the Church of San Damiano (which Francis had repaired some years earlier) with one of Clare's sisters, who also took the habit. Together, they began the community called the Order of Poor Ladies of San Damiano, popularly known as the "Poor Clares." Clare began a historic journey that would see her found monasteries in Italy, France and Germany. The nuns wore no stockings, went barefoot, slept on the ground, begged for their food and never owned property. Eventually, Francis moderated these excessive practices. He counselled Clare to sleep on a mattress and eat something each day, if only a piece of bread. Clare believed that she, along with her sisters, always had what they needed, even though they always had little.

*

What do you desire in life? What material things will bring you that extra edge of happiness? A moment of reflection might surface both small and large desires. But in the end, God has given us all we need, as Clare of Assisi recognized with her nuns so many centuries ago. Perhaps we need to open our eyes and our hearts to see how this is true in our lives.

A scientist and farmer went camping. They both went to sleep, and the farmer woke up several hours later. She immediately elbowed the scientist and said, "Wake up! What do you see?" The scientist responded, "Millions of stars!" – and proceeded to name several constellations and other astronomical features of the sky. The farmer interjected when she couldn't take it anymore: "You idiot! Somebody stole our tent!" Sometimes we need to see the obvious in our lives and not look for anything too complicated. Perhaps we do have everything we need after all.

The stories of God's care in the scriptures are simple. Both in the Hebrew Bible and in the New Testament, these stories can be reflected upon to help alleviate our anxiety about obtaining what we believe we need more of. In the Book of Job, we read of our human dependency on God and how God cares for us: "In his hand is the life of every living thing and the breath of every human being." (Job 12:10)

In Matthew's Gospel we see God's testimony of care: "Look at the birds of the air; they neither sow nor reap nor gather into barns, and yet your heavenly Father feeds them. Are you not of more value than they?" (Matthew 6:26)

Keeping this in mind, we need to be cautious about what we pray for. Remember the cry of the Israelite people to the Lord that they be delivered from their captivity and slavery in Egypt: "But the people thirsted for water and the people complained against Moses and said, 'Why did you bring us out of Egypt, to kill us and our children and livestock with thirst?'" (Exodus 17:3)

The Israelites longed for their freedom; they longed to return to the land of their ancestors in Canaan (modern-day Israel). They had prayed to the Lord that the Egyptian Pharaoh would free them, and eventually the Pharaoh did. But, to follow this path of freedom to get what they wanted, they had to travel from Egypt to Canaan over treacherous desert lands and perilous mountain pathways. On this journey they endured deprivation and suffering. It took a long time – forty years. God gave them what they desired, but their freedom wasn't achieved instantly, and the journey involved personal investment and sacrifice.

God does not want us to suffer and does not cause suffering. But the pathway from where you are to where you want to be may require changes in your life that cause discomfort. It may require an investment of your time, a different way of looking at the world or yourself, and a new way of nurturing key relationships in your life. Change is not easy. We usually do need to suffer in some way to get what we desire. Along the way, we may need to look honestly at our lives and discern what is truly important, and then make the required changes.

God may not always be present to us in the ways we expect or want. Like the Israelites, we may get what we pray for and then want something different. This leads us again to consider the unfathomable way God is present to us, how God is making all things new – beyond our hopes, beyond our desires, beyond our expectations.

As baptized people, we are continually invited with Jesus to break through the usual, the expected, the norms of our time. In short, we are constantly challenged, in our prayers of wanting more or wanting change, to embrace life in a new way. As Jesus experienced the plenitude of God in his life, he too underwent radical suffering. He desired to be faithful to his long-standing relationship with God. To be faithful to that relationship, he had to follow a path he would rather have avoided. As he broke through and broke down many of the cultural norms of his day to achieve justice and equality, he experienced derision and rejection.

The same dynamic was at play when Jesus talked to the woman at the well. (John 4:1-10) Tired from his journey, he sat by the village well. Wells were busy places in those days – the source of life. Jesus met a woman there and asked her to give him some water. In doing so, he broke through two cultural and religious norms of his day: first, he dared to travel through a Samaritan town; second, he spoke in public to a woman who was not related to him. This was scandalous behaviour on both counts, and people criticized him greatly.

This meeting had the potential to redefine the relationship between those who belonged to society's mainstream, acceptable groups and those who didn't. It also had the potential to redefine the social status of women.

Like the woman at the well, our task is to go to the well to get what we want, to pray for what we desire. At the well, we bring our naked honesty – the full depth of our being. We meet the other in a moment of authentic encounter. Like the Israelites in the land of Egypt, we will be set free when we encounter ourselves in truth and honesty. Like the people of Israel and the woman at the well, we will receive living water so we may live abundantly. It is not things that we desire, but meaningful relationships that bring happiness and a sense of purpose.

Clare of Assisi is reported to have said:

We become what we love, and who we love shapes what we become. If we love things, we become a thing. If we love nothing, we become nothing. Imitation is not a literal mimicking of Christ, rather it means becoming the image of the beloved, an image disclosed through transformation. This means we are to become vessels of God's compassionate love for others.[15]

This desire is the deepest desire we can have for our life – to become wellsprings of the water of eternal life for others.

Ultimately, the water of eternal life that Jesus gives will break our bad habits – our ways of acting that keep us from encountering one another in truth or that reflect our personal shame or self-loathing. For we are also called to encounter ourselves in an authentic way, with all our past errors and sin.

This means we ought to pray for what we desire, but we need to be mindful that God may not answer in the way we expect. We need to go to the well of life within, to not be afraid to confront the poverty of our lives, for that is where we meet Jesus. Drink the water of truth and share your joy with others.

. . . .

Questions for Prayerful Reflection

1. What do you want out of life? What are you looking for? Name two or three goals that, if you were to achieve them, your happiness, purpose in life and personal well-being will have increased significantly. Does anything block you from achieving these goals? Name this and be present to it.

2. When it comes to material possessions, what do you believe will bring that extra edge of happiness to your life? Imagine that you have obtained these things. Do they really correlate to what you want out of life? Why or why not?

3. Do you believe that in God's eyes you have all you need? Why or why not?

4. Will anything you want to acquire or achieve require changes in your life, maybe even a major sacrifice or discomfort? What are these changes, and how can you reach out to others to support you in your journey? How is your Christian faith engaged in this journey of change?

Meditation Nine
The Christian Life of Prayer

Companion of the Meditation: Patron Saint of Students and Academics: Thomas Aquinas (1225–1274), Doctor of the Church

From a young age, Thomas benefited from a full education. Growing up in southern Italy near the small town of Aquino (about halfway between Rome and Naples), Thomas was the youngest of four sons and several daughters. Due to political unrest, his parents took him to a nearby monastery to live. There, he received formal schooling until he was about thirteen years old, when he went to the University of Naples to earn a degree in arts and science. At age nineteen, against the express wishes of his family, he joined the Dominicans, an order of men who travelled to preach in parishes. His studies continued in Cologne, Germany, and then in Paris. Eventually Thomas taught at several institutions himself. As a student Thomas was reserved and didn't talk much, so he was referred to as "the dumb Sicilian ox." But Thomas was anything but stupid – his intelligence eventually proved them all wrong. As a scholar he intervened in numerous debates concerning important questions of the day, winning over countless people to his positions. His books, particularly the *Summa theologiae*, became standard references for those studying theology, as they are to this day. Of interest was Thomas' use of the writings of Aristotle, a Greek philosopher of the fourth century BCE. Thomas had no problem recognizing wisdom and knowledge where it lies, whether within or outside the Christian tradition.

The New Testament contains many references to prayer. Most Christians are familiar with the Lord's Prayer. (Matthew 6:9-13; Luke 11:2-4) Saint Paul urged the Christian community in Thessalonica to "pray without ceasing." (1 Thessalonians 5:17) He admonished the community in Rome to "Rejoice in hope, be patient in suffering, persevere in prayer" (Romans 12:12), and the Ephesians to "Pray in the Spirit at all times in every prayer and supplication." (Ephesians 6:18) Clearly, prayer was essential to the life of the early Christians. It was also important to Jesus – he spent a good amount of time in prayer.

Before Jesus chose the twelve who would journey with him in a special way through the remainder of his life, he prayed to God and communed with God's Spirit. He took time away on a mountaintop and communed with God in silence. (Luke 6:12-13) Another key example is found in John's Gospel. All of chapter 17 recounts the prayer of Jesus. Jesus prays with God so that all of Jesus' followers may be one with God as he is one with God. For Jesus, prayer was an intimate expression of an existing relationship with God, as well as an expression of what Jesus desired for all people: oneness with God, which includes knowledge of God. One way we come to know God is through prayer. Thomas Aquinas wrote a brief prayer for this purpose:

> Grant me, O Lord my God, a mind to know you, a heart to seek you, wisdom to find you, conduct pleasing to you, faithful perseverance in waiting for you, and a hope of finally embracing you. Amen.

For Aquinas, one way of achieving oneness with God and getting to know God better was by having an ongoing conversation with God: Father, Son and Spirit. Jesus invites us to join in that conversation and works to draw us into it in a variety of ways. In Jesus' prayer, all people have been adopted into the life of the Trinity. Jesus wants us to have what he has with God – on the level of relationship and in the way we live our lives with each other.

Here is an example that concerns the type of justice God wants for us, that connects this justice with our life of prayer.

Jesus told a parable about a widow and an unjust judge. (Luke 18:1-8) The woman sought to be justified with her opponent before a judge, but he refused to hear her plea. Time and again she returned to plead her case. Finally, the judge relented. In response, Jesus said, "And will not God grant justice to his chosen ones who cry to him day and night? Will he delay long in helping them? I tell you, he will quickly grant justice to them." Jesus encourages us to pray always and not to lose faith in our prayer before God. Keep the conversation going, he tells us, just as he kept the conversation with God going through all the years Jesus lived among us.

But what is prayer? How do we do it? And then the kicker: Why is it that prayers, even in urgent and dire circumstances, are not always answered the way we would like? After all, the passage from Luke cited above tells us that "justice will come."

This reflection on prayer reminds me of a friend who is a real estate agent. She depends on her income from selling houses to support her family. My friend told me of a colleague who prayed to God to sell more houses. His prayers were answered; he did sell more houses! My friend tried the same thing, but her business did not increase, so she phoned me to ask me what she was doing wrong.

What she failed to realize is that prayer is not a matter of cause and effect. Prayer should help us detach from the idea of concrete outcomes. This is what Jesus did when he prayed. He knew that God is always in us, around us, above and below us. Prayer is the awareness that living in God's presence is the Christian reality. To be aware of God's intimate and abiding presence is already to be deeply engaged in prayer. "Saying our prayers" is meant to sensitize us to this presence, to deepen it and to make us aware of how God loves us and transforms our lives through everyday experiences. What greater gift could we want than to commit our time and energy to being aware of the Divine Spirit in our heart, our soul and our life?

Origen of Alexandria wrote about Christian prayer in the third century. He taught that the entire lives of those who closely follow the teachings and spirit of Jesus Christ are prayer. For Origen, prayer was not something we do; it is a lifestyle.

That prayer is a lifestyle focused on nurturing the conscious presence of God in our lives makes sense of Paul's admonition to "pray always" – to always live in the presence and mind of God. Prayer is not a constant repetition of formulas of praise, petition or pious practices. It is about developing a sense of interiority where our actions, hopes and desires touch God's life. Prayer is always answered in that it never fails to deepen our relationships with God and with others. Prayer springs from a foundation of care for others and, in the praying, strengthens that foundation. Our prayers and the prayers of others are answered when the blind see a new life, the disillusioned experience hope, quarrelling becomes peace and the sinner sins no more. In this way, the words Jesus taught us to pray are fulfilled: God's kingdom comes "on earth as it is in heaven."

My moral life is part of my prayer: how I am and how I act before the other is an expression of prayer. Because I am not one with the other yet, nor one with God, I need to reflect on my life of prayer, of being God's *pray-er* for the other. Because I fail in this relationship periodically and I sin, reflecting on my sin should also be considered part of my prayer. Prayer opens the door to the realization that our hearts have been broken and that we have broken the hearts of others. Yet God loves us through all of this.

Mechthild von Magdeburg, a devout Christian woman of the thirteenth century who lived in what is now Germany, describes the experience of relationship with God this way:

> Of what are you made, soul, that you rise so high over all creatures, and mingle with the holy Trinity and yet remain wholly in yourself? – You have spoken of my origin, now I tell it to you truly: I was made in that place from love, therefore no creature can satisfy me according to my noble nature, and no creature can unlock me, except love alone.[16]

Mechthild speaks of the origin of human life, which is birthed from Divine Love. Although in birth, human life is separated from its origins in God, it also has its own noble vocation: to live in and through Divine Love. Thomas Aquinas described this as living a virtuous life; a life of faith, hope and charity. From this dynamic, the fullness of human life is achieved. Human life is oriented from the beginning to live that "noble" life of which Mechthild speaks. Prayer is awareness of our participation in Divine Love, mingling with the Trinity in life as we know it today. In prayer, we surrender to the draw of God's love and enter more fully into an awareness of God's desire for us.

Thomas Aquinas was a contemplative, and some suggest he was a mystic. But for him, contemplation meant being fully involved in every dimension of life. Christian prayer takes us to the heart of the action. Prayer is not a distraction from life, but the mindful (prayerful) centering of our lives in being God-become-flesh for others.

Through Jesus' prayer, God transformed his moments of suffering and joy into opportunities for the salvation of others. Jesus was God's *pray-er* for us. This is what our prayer life ought to lead to: we become God's *pray-er* for others. Let us end this meditation on prayer with a prayer written by our companion saint, Thomas Aquinas:

Give us, O Lord, a steadfast heart, which no
unworthy affection may drag downwards;
give us an unconquered heart, which no tribulation
can wear out;
give us an upright heart, which no unworthy
purpose may tempt aside.

Bestow upon us also, O Lord our God,
understanding to know you,
diligence to seek you, wisdom to find you,
and a faithfulness that may finally embrace you;
through Jesus Christ our Lord.[17]

. . . .

Questions for Prayerful Reflection

1. Do I separate my prayer life from everyday life? Do I see my spiritual life as independent from my everyday activities? If so, what can I do to unite my prayer with my daily life?

2. How does my prayer reflect a "cause and effect" attitude? If I pray to God for something or to bless/heal another and it does not come about, how do I feel about this? What attitude(s) might I consider changing for my prayer to be transformed from expecting specific outcomes to helping me become one with the other?

3. Prayer helps us become aware of our weaknesses so we can transform them into strengths. What sins of my past might form the raw material for my strengths of the future? What do I need to do to make this transformation real?

4. What difference does it make, if any, to pray with others rather than by myself? How might my prayer help me become more aware of God's presence in the lives of others today?

Meditation Ten

Care of the Body: We Are God's Flesh

Companion of the Meditation: Patron Saint of Lovers: Valentine (226–269)

Valentine is a saint celebrated in several liturgical traditions – for example, Lutheran, Catholic and Anglican. This is unusual given the scarcity and ambiguity of information relating to him. Born in Rome at the time of an intense Roman persecution, Valentine spent a good amount of his time helping those in need and was faced with the threat of death. Eventually he, too, met the wrath of the Roman emperor and was beheaded. It is difficult to confirm this account of Valentine's life because two Valentines lived at the same time in the region of Rome – one a priest, the other a bishop. Although it is difficult to establish the authentic details of the life of Saint Valentine, his following was real and continues to this day. The tradition of celebrating young lovers on Valentine's Day arose much later in history. In the 1400s, it was noted that birds began to pair on February 14, the springtime of the year. Young men followed suit by sending a note to their chosen "Valentine" on this day.

What does it mean to say that God has taken on human flesh? This question is important, since Christianity has a history of demeaning the body and exalting the spirit. But the Song of Songs – a biblical love poem expressing the intimate relationship between a man and a woman – shows that the Bible celebrates the experience of the body as well as the physical love between two people. It is this spirit of love that is also celebrated by Saint Valentine and the Christian tradition on Valentine's Day. So we see mixed messages concerning the body in the history of Christianity.

Too often, the body as flesh has been pitted against the soul as spirit – and the spirit is often seen as more important. The reasons for this division and exaltation of spirit over body might be many. However, a misreading of scripture (including the Song of Songs) may be one cause of separating body from spirit, as if they exist in two independent worlds.

Let's take, as an example, a text from Paul's first letter to the Corinthians, where he contrasts a "spiritual" person with an "unspiritual" person. (1 Corinthians 2:14–3:3) Paul says those who are unspiritual do not receive the gifts of God's Spirit, while those who are spiritual do receive these gifts, see clearly and are mindful of God's ways.

Paul goes on to say that the jealousy and quarrelling among the people of Corinth shows they are "of the flesh"; that is, they are unspiritual. For Paul, such people are animated by a life of self-indulgence, quarrels and jealousy. (We see this in Galatians 5:19-21.) Paul refers to an unspiritual person as a "natural" person, since they give in to their unbridled impulses, which results in a life of strife and division. Paul describes this life-style as a life of flesh – a life that is not guided by God's Spirit.

A spiritual person, however, lives a life guided by God's Spirit, a life of "love, joy, peace, patience, kindness, generosity, faithfulness, gentleness and self-control." (Galatians 5:22)

In contrasting the life of flesh with a life of spirit, Paul was not speaking of any opposition between *body* and *spirit*, that is, between the flesh and the soul. He was speaking to the people about two different ways of living. Living in the Spirit referred to living one's life discerning the call of God in one's heart, directed toward the love of others. Living in the flesh referred to living one's life without regard to this call of God and disregarding the lives of others.

If this is what Paul was getting at – and there is good reason to believe that this is the case – he was not opposing the body and the spirit. Rather, they belong together as one: all of a person's attributes are needed to live fully in the Spirit. Human body/flesh and human soul/spirit are so enmeshed, they form one locus for the in-breaking of God in the world. Paul taught his communities to live their entire life and bring their entire being under the impulse of God. This is what Jesus strove to do. He spent his three years of ministry teaching us to do the same under the guidance of the Spirit of God.

Unfortunately, Christian tradition, particularly from the twelfth century on, interpreted Paul's use of the word "flesh" as referring to the physical body instead of as a lifestyle that contravened God's hopes and dreams for us. Meanwhile, the word "spirit," as used by Paul, began to refer exclusively to the human soul. As a result, "flesh" or "body" began to be used with strong negative connotations, while "spirit" or "soul" was seen as positive. The body was thus demeaned, and the spirit was exalted.

Spiritual life was divorced from bodily life. Spirit was good; body was bad – as if one's physical body had no role in living a Spirit-filled Christian life. But the Christian tradition went further; it established an antagonistic relationship between body/flesh and spirit/soul. Paul's holistic teaching that all of one's life – as *one* entity – is to be guided by God's Spirit was lost.

As an adolescent and young adult, I remember experiencing all the tension and guilt surrounding the temptations that stemmed from my developing sexuality. I was often tortured by my struggles between what I understood to be body/flesh life and spirit/soul life. It was not acceptable to talk much about these things – except in the confessional. As a Catholic, the rift between body life and soul life was felt most acutely there: the confessional grille symbolized that the "holy" resided on one side of the grille and the "not so holy" on the other. Through the grille I could literally see the light while I knelt in darkness.

Today, in the Christian traditions, we are rediscovering what Paul meant. Christian life is the life of the Incarnation. God, through the person of Jesus, took on human flesh – real human flesh and blood. God did this as an expression of God's love for the world – all of it. This is a good way to view the celebration of Saint Valentine's Day. God's spiritual intimacy with us comes through wholesome and loving relationships that are expressed physically. God loved us and the world through Jesus in an embodied way. God loved in the flesh as God expects us now to love in the spirit of Saint Paul's teaching.

Christianity and other religious traditions provide many examples that we can look to in order to find alternative ways of appreciating our bodies. There, the body is an integral part of expressing, nurturing and celebrating God in our lives. For example, King David celebrated the arrival of the ark of the Lord in his town by "leaping and dancing." His entire household "shouted" with joy in the streets. (2 Samuel 6) Julian of Norwich, a prominent English Christian mystic of the fourteenth century, expressed the value of the body in this way: "For as the body is clad in clothes, and the flesh in skin, and the bones in flesh, and the heart in the breast, so are we, soul and body, clad and enclosed in the goodness of God."[18]

Rābi'ah was a Muslim woman who founded Islamic mysticism in the eighth century. Within this tradition developed Sufis, commonly known as "whirling dervishes," who danced at funerals. Through movement and bodily gestures, Sufis got in touch with the mystery of God that they felt in their hearts. The body/self was experienced as one. One Sufi is known to have said, pointing to his cloak, "There is nothing in that cloak except Allah."

The body God has gifted us with is not shameful. God took on a body, robing it in the person of Jesus of Nazareth, and God now robes this body with our lives. The expression of Christian joy is to be found in the language of our bodies. Spontaneous, soul-filled exaltation and cup-brimming-full happiness are the hallmarks of Christian life. God came to give us life to the fullest. In this body, every day, all day long, God embraces us with the warmth of a thousand hugs given all at once. We ought to behave more often like children who jump, dance, throw around their arms and squeal with delight when they see one small thing that excites them. How much more excitement can there be in one's life than to discover the deep and abiding presence of God within? Yet, we hold back.

We are still recovering from the negative influence of misreading Paul's texts and a tradition that has emphasized spiritual life disassociated from bodily life. In unconscious ways, we live our daily lives harbouring a negative attitude toward this world – the world that God and humans share. We subtly separate matter and spirit, soul and body, natural and supernatural, heaven and earth. Our hearts thus are heavy.

It is a mistake to think the body and the physical world are devoid of spiritual meaning – that those who aspire to holiness must first escape the body to reach their spiritual goal. A healthy spiritual life has no such split. All of one's body/self is honoured, enjoyed and loved. Indeed, all of one's body/self is the vehicle of love, both to give and to receive. As such, our body is a revelation of God's being-in-the-world, in whose image we are joyfully created.

Questions for Prayerful Reflection

1. How has my attitude toward my body changed over time? Can I point to specific instances where I have undervalued or disdained my physical body in order to exalt the "spiritual" aspects of my life?

2. Do I separate my physical body from the grace God gives in my spiritual life, especially in my prayer life? How do my habits or practices denigrate the body (perhaps unconsciously) and treat it as less important in my spiritual and prayer life?

3. How could I intentionally incorporate my physical body into my Christian life? (For example, can I incorporate

body movements into my prayer life or become intentional about how I reflect God's image physically and spiritually?)

4. Pause for a moment in silence and be present to what is happening in your body right now. Take several slow deep breaths and listen. How would you describe your physical self-awareness in this moment?

Meditation Eleven

Asceticism as a Way to Engage Our Desires

....

Companion of the Meditation: Kateri Tekakwitha,
Protectress of Canada (1656–1680)

Kateri was born in the Mohawk village of Ossernenon, west of the current town of Auriesville, New York. Her parents named her Tekakwitha (meaning "she who bumps into things"). Orphaned at the age of four due to the death of her parents and brother when smallpox swept through their village, she was raised by members of her extended family. She took the name Kateri after Saint Catherine of Siena (Kateri was the Mohawk form of "Catherine") when she was baptized at the age of nineteen. Her decision to become Christian was unpopular with the villagers where she lived. Within a couple of years, in 1677, she moved to Kahnawake, a small mission run by the Jesuits on the St. Lawrence River south of Montreal. A devout Christian who did not marry, Kateri tended to the sick and elderly. Her desire was to give her life fully to God. She came to be known as the "Lily of the Mohawks." Kateri is the first Indigenous woman saint of the United States and Canada. She was born on one side of the border and died on the other. Kateri continues to inspire women and men due to her gentle good humour, holiness and respect for nature.[19]

The word "asceticism" may conjure up contrasting images.[20] From severe bodily deprivation to the solitary life of the monk or nun living behind monastery walls, Christian asceticism is one of the most misunderstood terms in the Christian vocabulary. It is easy to find pictures on the internet of people sporting signs of extreme bodily mortifications that some deem necessary to achieve Christian perfection. Although discouraged by local Catholic bishops, Good Friday processions in the Philippines still feature bloodied men flagellating themselves and wearing crowns of real thorns in imitation of Christ's passion. Or, think of movies such as *The Da Vinci Code* (2006), where members of a Catholic community known as Opus Dei are pictured wearing tight metallic belts fitted with metal spurs that dig into the flesh as a form of ascetical practice.

If we only consider these examples, it seems Christian asceticism means renouncing the pleasures of life and seeking physical pain for its own sake. This could not be further from the truth. Christianity values the world of the Incarnation and the world of the physical body. Kateri Tekakwitha is an example of this.

Life was difficult for Kateri, but she did not look for suffering. Her Christian values taught her to care for the sick, the elderly and those less fortunate. She was continually rebuked by her family and culture for her decision to become Christian. Asceticism for Kateri took the form of a commitment to Christian values, not a rebuke of this world or of her body.

What is asceticism if it is not a renunciation of physical pleasure, and why should we be concerned about it when reflecting on what we desire in life? As Christians, we reflect on the gift of the Incarnation, of divine life taking on human flesh, as how God embodied God's love for the material world. Let's look at the origins of the word "asceticism" to help us understand this.

The word finds its origins in the ancient Greek word *askesis*, which had to do with training or discipline. This term was originally used to describe the training athletes and soldiers underwent. Not only was the body conditioned, but so were their minds and their desires. This may have involved a range of choices – some of them uncomfortable – to achieve a high degree of physical fitness.

To appreciate Christian asceticism, consider the ebb and flow of the lives of people across the globe, regardless of whether they are religious believers.

Like the ancient Greeks, and like Kateri, people today constantly face choices as they strive to achieve their goals. All paths cannot be followed; people need to make choices if they are to attain their important life goals. For example, if a single parent on a low income who supports two children wants to set aside financial resources so the children can attend college later in life, important choices will need to be made. She will need to limit nights out to save on entertainment, babysitting and transportation costs. This may mean giving up time with friends – not because this is bad or destructive, but because another long-term goal is guiding her. Parenting is a kind of asceticism. In any life, choices need to be made among competing interests; this is a kind of asceticism. Asceticism helps people find a balance among competing desires or needs.

If desires get out of control and propel some people toward destructive self-indulgent behaviours, they may choose not to act on those desires to achieve their other goals. We are often lured in directions that have no substance. Asceticism – understood as making intentional and wise choices to avoid excess, to consider more than the immediate moment – is necessary for a person to mature. People never stop becoming who they desire to be; the fullness of human life is not realizable once and for all. The whole of human life, over many years, requires an asceticism that shapes feelings and actions to help people realize the deepest aspirations of the human heart. Many religious traditions hold this to be true.

The conventions of Buddhists, Muslims, Jews, Hindus and Christians include a range of ascetic disciplines. Muslims, for instance, observe a rigorous fast in the month of Ramadan, during which they refrain from sensual pleasures between sunrise and sundown. Buddhist monks refrain from attending shows and entertainments, sleeping on luxurious beds, having sexual intercourse and possessing money. Christians observe ascetical practices such as prayer, fasting and the sharing of material resources with those in need, especially during the forty days of Lent. These practices are part of Christians' spiritual preparation for Easter.

Asceticism does not mean renouncing the pleasures of life or practising harsh physical punishments for their own sake. Christian asceticism is a positive movement toward fulfilment in life, a realization of one's deepest hopes and dreams for one's own life, the lives of loved ones and the life of the world – God's world. Christian asceticism includes the choices we make to achieve appropriate human relationships. But those practices are performed with the eyes of faith, knowing that it is God who calls us forth and gives us the strength to make what may be difficult decisions.

Although done personally, asceticism is never done alone; it is done in relationship with the Christian community, in particular with the worshipping community, whose members choose to share more fully in the life of God. Just as Jesus made choices that led to his death in order to open the possibility of resurrection for all, Christian asceticism participates in this same journey of dying and rising to new life. In a special way, therefore, the Eucharistic celebration (the Mass) is the ascetic feast par excellence. There, living, dying and rising come full circle in the blessing, breaking and sharing of the Body of Christ. We live, die and rise as one just as Jesus is one with God. Christians shape an ascetic Eucharistic community to journey with one another, because the ambiguities of life and human desire can lead us astray individually.

Human desire can fall prey to the trap of excessive indulgence in life, to the false hopes contained in empty promises, and the powerful forces of cultural or popular movements. In a consumer society, we desire to have more, and we are drowning in the excesses of our own desires. We sometimes lose our way amid the range of choices available in our quest for happiness and meaning. A program of asceticism assists in our task of becoming more of who we want to be. Christian asceticism aims at the transformation of human desire itself. It helps break us out of the narrow boundaries within which we tend to root our desires for life.

For the sake of growth, Christians place boundaries on some of our ambiguous desires – for example, the misuse of sexuality, unjust possessions, manipulative power or abusive relationships. The love of God and neighbour requires practice until we get it right – well, as right as we can in the world as we know it. What is tarnished in our lives needs polishing from time to time.

Asceticism refreshes and perfects the *imago Dei*, the image of God, in which we were created. This refreshing happens in the ordinary experiences of life; we need not look far to find opportunities. Christian asceticism awakens and transforms the heart of humanity to God's grace. This takes patience; we cannot rush God's work. Everything grows at its own pace – be it a butterfly coming out of its cocoon or a human being.

Like the birthing of a butterfly, Christian asceticism is lived patiently in the daily encounter with our brothers and sisters. Yes, we need to grow and be intentional about it, but it is not helpful to hurry that which needs more time. We need to be patient with our own unfolding.

This approach to asceticism challenges the common assumption that Christian asceticism, interpreted as corporal punishment or as a complete renunciation of human sexuality or sensuality, has little or nothing to offer us today.

The above reflection helps us recognize the wisdom of the tradition of healthy Christian asceticism practised through the ages. Christian asceticism ought to help the believer make responsible and life-giving choices that respond positively to daily ups and downs, while recognizing God's graceful presence in our activities. We are invited to explore all the goods God has set before us, the spiritual as well as the sensual. But ascetical practices help to keep it all in balance.

Questions for Prayerful Reflection

1. How did you understand the word "asceticism" before reading the above meditation? Has your understanding changed? If so, how?

2. Name two or three goals in your life for which you will need to practise "asceticism": that is, make choices that will deny you other options that are also good.

3. Name two or three bad habits you have developed that you need to reconsider so you can polish and refresh the *imago Dei* in which you were created. What ascetic practices might you do to minimize those bad habits or leave them behind? When will you take the first steps?

Meditation Twelve
My Call to Leadership

Companion of the Meditation: Patron Saint of Catholic Action: Francis of Assisi (1181/82–1226)

The wondrous life of the Italian Francis of Assisi has attracted widespread admiration, not only from Christians, but from individuals and communities of a range of faith traditions or of no faith at all. Francis captured the imagination of his time by describing the three vows which he took as a monk – poverty, chastity and obedience – in terms of troubadours (poets who roamed the countryside singing and playing folksongs) and songs of courtly love (songs of passionate love of a knight for his lady). So much in love with poverty was Francis that he referred to his marriage to "Lady Poverty." His love of nature is unsurpassed – perhaps even to this day. His parents were well off and he spent money lavishly. He did, however, even from his youth, extend alms to the poor when asked. While riding his horse one day, he encountered a leper whose sores were so loathsome that the leper repelled all he encountered. But Francis dismounted his horse, and as the leper stretched out his hands for alms, Francis kissed him while giving him some money. This was a turning point in his life; Francis henceforth assumed a new orientation. He visited hospitals often and served the sick. Eventually, along with a few others, he settled in a small cottage outside the gates of Assisi. Out of this humble beginning came the worldwide congregation known as the Franciscans. Francis is also credited with entrenching the custom of the Christmas "crib" – the display of the baby Jesus in his own humble beginnings.

Christianity is full of men and women who became leaders like Francis of Assisi. They were so in love with God and had such a passion for life that they influenced many to live with the same spirit. The Bible also tells many stories of men and women whom God called into various forms of leadership: for example, David, who defended the Israelites against the Philistines. (1 Samuel 17) David, a young man with only a slingshot, defeated the mighty Goliath who was large in stature and wore heavy armour. David went on to become king of his people. Then there was Deborah (Judges 4–5), a prophet and judge. She also led the army of ancient Israel. The disciple Paul of Tarsus speaks of two women, Euodia and Syntyche, as his co-workers. (Philippians 4:2) They helped him to spread the gospel. Leaders who defended the rights of others, spoke the truth of God or spread the good news of Jesus abound in the Bible.

What do these leaders have in common? For the most part they were ordinary folk from ordinary circumstances who were called to do marvellous things because they had the heart of God. We may not see ourselves as leaders because we may not see ourselves as having the heart of God. However, we need to remind ourselves that God does not see human beings as we see ourselves: "mortals ... look on the outward appearance, but the Lord looks on the heart." (1 Samuel 16:7) In raising up David to be king of the Israelites, for example, God chose the one whom others thought was the least: a young boy who tended sheep in the fields.

God has a deep knowledge of each person – a knowledge that always leads to God loving that person even more. Leadership comes from within, from the core of our passions, interests and commitments. Christian leadership comes from the solid conviction that faith in God comes before all else; faith guides all one's decisions and actions. Once Francis realized this, he didn't let anything stop him from giving his life totally to God.

I am reminded of a man I worked with while I was in Haiti teaching high school. Valbrun was the father of six children. Like David, he was a herdsman; he tended goats and gardens in the village where I lived. Valbrun was slight in stature and rough in appearance. I remember not thinking highly of him in our first encounters. I mistakenly judged the book by its cover. After a while, I came to know him as a wise and noble man. He gave me much good counsel during the time I knew him, and I came to count on the practical advice he generously offered. I return to that experience when I feel I may again be hastily judging a person.

God sees beyond our external and internal dispositions. God sees beyond our attempts to manipulate, judge or reduce others to superficial impressions. As a result of our short-sightedness, we hurt others despite our desire not to do so. But God knows us as we are.

God's focus is on our beauty and grace as human beings. Leadership is not based on externals or on greatness as we understand it. Most people do not publicly achieve goals recognized as extraordinary. But public recognition is not what life is about. Christian leadership is focused on the conviction that God is in this world, causing great things to happen in our everyday encounters – in our authentic encounter with others and recognition of their human dignity. There can be no greater leadership. After all, Jesus spent his whole life encountering others as they were – sinners and saints alike. He encountered them in table fellowship, at the public wells of the villages he visited and as he travelled the dusty roads of Galilee.

We are all called to leadership wherever we find ourselves, regardless of our age, our current disposition or our abilities. We may not do things as great and daring as King David did, but we can do beautiful things with whomever we meet. We also need to believe that others can do beautiful things. We must never yield to the temptation to judge, jump to conclusions or dismiss others. As God chose the last, the one discarded, the improbable one, so too are we invited to give the benefit of the doubt to our brothers and sisters. We are invited to allow the other to contribute their gifts – however small they may be in our eyes – for they will be great in the eyes of God. This is what it means to be *enlightened*.

The story of the healing of the blind man in John's Gospel (9:1-41) helps us better understand this. Jesus says, "this man was born blind so that God's work might be revealed." (John 9:3) Again, as we saw in the scripture stories at the beginning of this meditation, the one who is less, who has less ability, is chosen to do God's work – to be a leader. In contrast to the one who cannot see, that is, the one who sits in darkness, Jesus declares himself to be the "light of the world." (John 9:5) The light of Jesus is the force in leadership, in decision making, in finding our way through complex, problematic situations.

This helps us realize we should not sweat the small stuff. Too often our energy is used in fretting about things that do not have a serious impact on our lives and those we love. Irritating situations do affect us. But when our time and energy are dedicated to minor issues, we limit our ability to attend to the issues that truly matter. By becoming preoccupied with little things, we miss the opportunity to nurture the conditions for true leadership – moments where we help the light of Jesus shine in this world.

I am reminded of Etty Hillesum, a Jewish woman, whose story of leadership is one of the most inspiring of our times. Etty lived in Amsterdam during the Second World War; she began assisting refugees at a transit camp in the summer of 1942. These transit camps, built by the Nazis, held Jewish people and other "undesirables" (such as people with mental or physical disabilities, as well as homosexuals) while they awaited transport to an extermination camp.

Etty gave generously of herself, aiding those in Camp Westerbork who needed food, clothing, comfort and friendship. Most of all, she desired to give friendship – a kind of leadership we are all capable of giving. At first, she was free to move in and out of the camp, but eventually, when she was twenty-nine, Nazi officials sent her to Auschwitz, where she died in the death chambers on November 30, 1943.

Etty, along with Francis, King David, Deborah, Paul, Euodia, Syntyche, Valbrun and the blind man in John's Gospel, challenges us to assume the mantle of self-giving love. All these figures challenge us to reach out to others, not because of their outer appearance or weaknesses, but for who they are in themselves. We all carry the scars of a thousand hurts and failures. From those wounds shine the mercy and love of God. From those wounds we touch the hearts of others, as those leaders did. But they had to choose to do so. They had to lead themselves before they inspired others to lead in a similar way.

Mercy is the capacity to enter the chaos and misery, as well as the joy and blessedness, of the life of another human being, such that they too enter into *our* chaos and *our* happiness. In doing so, we satisfy their longing for life, their deepest search for meaning in life. Mercy is finding a way to satisfy the hunger of another. It means we take the risk of losing control of our own lives to truly be with the other. We need to choose to lead our own self in this way. Perhaps then we will lead others to do the same.

Mercy is intimately linked to compassion. In Hebrew, the word for "compassion" is *rechem*, which means womb. It comes from the root *racham*, which means compassion and mercy. To be compassionate, to show mercy, is to create a womb-like space in our lives for others so they will be able to find new life.

This is the leadership we are being asked to grow into as Christians. Can we truly be that womb-like space that others seek? Compassion is about becoming a homeless shelter for others. In the words of Etty Hillesum, we do this wherever we find ourselves at this moment:

Sometimes I long for a convent cell, with the sublime wisdom of centuries set out on bookshelves all along the wall and a view across the cornfields – there must be cornfields and they must wave in the breeze – and there I would immerse myself in the wisdom of the ages and in myself. Then I might perhaps find peace and clarity. But that would be no great feat. It is right here, in this very place, in the here and the now, that I must find them.[21]

. . . .

Questions for Prayerful Reflection

1. What do I imagine when I think of a leader? Can I identify some people I know who reflect these qualities?

2. Do I think I am too old to be a true leader? Too young? Too unskilled? Why do I consider these as blocks if leadership is primarily a way of living authentic values that inspire others to do the same?

3. Think of your own leadership style – the way you influence people through your actions and the way you are present to them. When you have an influence on others, what is it that others find attractive?

Meditation Thirteen

Sin as a Sign of God's Original Blessing

....

Companions of the Meditation: Patron Saints of Farmers
and Rural Communities – Maria Torribia (died 1175)
and Isidore the Husbandman (died 1130)

sidore the Husbandman was born in the Spanish capital,
Madrid, to poor parents who were people of great faith.
They could not afford a proper education for their son, but
they instilled in him a love of prayer, a passion for the faith
and a horror of sin. Once he was old enough, Isidore began
work as a farm labourer. He spent his time ploughing the fields
and attending to the blessings of the harvest. Isidore married
Maria Torribia; they had one son who died at a young age.
Isidore and Maria are a model of married life. Although they
lived during a time starkly different than ours, they faced the
same issues many couples face today: attending to their mutual
support, providing for a family and experiencing the blessings
of self-giving sacrificial love. Isidore and Maria, though poor
themselves, shared generously with others. After his day's
work, Isidore often brought home those who were hungry to
share their meagre meal. Maria was beatified in 1697 and is

honoured in Spain as Santa Maria de la Cabeza. The virtues found in the lives of Isidore and Maria – love of family, respect for nature and the land, generosity to the poor – are still alive and well in farmlands around the world.

Prayer for Farm Families in Crisis

O God, our costs are up and prices for our produce down. The loan is due, and there's no money to buy this year's seed. We feel alone, embarrassed in our need, like failures in our efforts to farm.

The harder we work, the worse it seems to get. There's no laughter or joy anymore, just a constant struggle to believe, to hope and to keep trying. Strengthen us, God.

Keep us gentle and yet firm, generous yet open to receive. Let us see your face in those who want to help and don't know how. Grant us perseverance and openness to your will.

Hold our family close as we do our best to know and act according to your will in the days ahead. We ask this through Christ our Lord. Amen.[22]

The story of creation is found in the Book of Genesis, the first book of the Bible. We read that God formed human beings from the dirt of the earth and breathed God's Spirit into them to give life. From the beginning, God's Spirit animated and directed human life. Further, humanity was given the means to live and flourish in the beautiful Garden of Eden. Plenty was given so life could sustain itself and human beings could be free to live in harmony with God. Isidore and Maria, the companion saints for this meditation, were in tune with this reality as they ploughed the earth and reaped the earth's blessings.

Like the story of Isidore and Maria, the story from Genesis affirms that our life is from God. From the start, life owes its existence to God's initiative. God desired to share the life God experienced with the Eternal Word (Jesus) and God's Spirit with human beings, who were fashioned in God's likeness. We also see that human beings were placed in a world and a life of blessings. All that was needed not only for sustenance, but for happiness, was provided. God also gave human beings the freedom to choose right from wrong.

As the story continues in Genesis, we learn that the gift of freedom can be exercised in different ways – some helpful, others not. Some decisions resulted in the destruction of the relationships that God had given as part of God's gift – relationships among persons, between persons and the beautiful world, and between persons and God. The abuse and breakdown of these relationships resulted in what we call sin. Along with God's original blessing, we carry in our hearts the mark of sin. Sin is a stark reminder of the transcendent gift of freedom given to us at the beginning. Thus sin and blessing go hand in hand. Augustine of Hippo, an early Christian writer who died in 430 CE in northern Africa, holds this position. In Book XIII of his *City of God*, Augustine says that "from the bad use of free will," sin entered the world and enslaved humanity.[23]

He talks about "the soul revelling in its own liberty" and losing its way as a result. We can learn much from this insight.

With Augustine we can describe sin as the tendency to stretch God's blessings – God's gift of free will – to the point of rupture. As such, sin is the tendency to separate ourselves from the fullness of life. We stretch power and authority to the point that it is not power for and with our beloved sister and brother, but power over and against them. We stretch knowledge to the point where it is no longer at the service of others, but a source of manipulation and control. We stretch the goods of the earth to the point where they are no longer at the service of life and sustenance for all, but are rather a means whereby some are kept in servitude for the material benefit of others.

We stretch the original blessings of life to the point where they are no longer blessings but the cause of separation of people from each other, from the earth and from God. This is the core identity of sin. In sin we stretch the capacities God has given us to the point where we rupture the image of God, in whose likeness we were made. The original image, the original blessing, can be described as a blessing of harmony among all, of self-giving, and of care and concern for self, others, world and God.

As a result of the tendency to stretch God's original blessings, power becomes oppressive, knowledge becomes a tool for enslavement and abuse, and the goods of the earth become the source of economic inequality and injustice. Although God's original blessings are good in themselves, we sin in the way we use them. This is far from the humble gratitude and service lived by Isidore and Maria, who used the blessings they were given to nourish those they met.

That's why it is a good idea to examine our freedoms: to understand how we have caused them to flip and become our unfreedoms. Here we bump against a paradox of the human condition: our God-given freedom causes us to be unfree in so many ways. Another way of saying this is that *sin is a mark of our freedom.* Sin, falling short of all the goods of the creator God, helps us understand the nature of the original blessings with which we are endowed.

We are slaves to our own blindness and need to find how to see again with clarity, light and truth, as Jesus did. We need to look deep inside and see how we are unfree, discover sin in our lives and reorient ourselves along the pathway of right relationship in tune with God's original blessings. On this journey, we pick up our cross.

The cross is the place of transformation and conversion, the place of crossing from unfreedom to freedom. Many times, this transition is painful because we are moving from what is known to the unknown, from old ways to new ways. The real problem is not that we sin, but that we do not sin enough. What does this mean? How can we say, "We do not sin enough"? Does this not contradict the journey of life in God that Jesus desired to reveal in his own life?

"We do not sin enough" means *we are not aware* of our daily transgressions: the ways our hurtful comments and actions, our subtle abuses of power, our manipulation of knowledge and our use of goods offends, diminishes or shames the other. The end effect of these transgressions is a separation from the original blessing of harmony and togetherness with which we have been gifted. "We do not sin enough" because we are not aware of how we really operate in the world. If we did, we would know that we do sin more. Even with all our noble intentions, we diminish the image of God in our lives through behaviours that divide rather than foster harmony. A hard look at ourselves may help us discover our blindness and thus to free our brothers and sisters from our well-intentioned but tyrannical ways.

The task is to discover our unfreedoms so our brothers and sisters can be free from our blindness and no longer shackled by our shortcomings. We need to fast more. Fasting from our unfreedoms is a practice we ought to be engaged in throughout the year. We need to fast from all that hurts and holds those around us in bondage. We need to fast from deceitful behaviour, the desire for retribution, putting down the other and gossiping about the other.

Fasting in this way will help us ensure that our power empowers others, our knowledge grows into wisdom and our unfreedom becomes a source of others' freedom. As we look within our lives, we should not be afraid to try new behaviours, adopt new attitudes and share more of what we possess. Fasting intentionally in this way is an opportunity to leave behind the old self, the tired self, the self held in bondage so that we and others may be free. We have all known the loneliness that results from unjust treatment, from the burden of less-than-wise choices and from treating others as less than grace-filled human beings.

We experience captivity in many ways. Sometimes it is from external structures. But more often, and more importantly, it is from within. We need to exercise a self-care modelled on God's care for us. In this way we can live this care in truth-filled relationships with our brothers and sisters. We are called to feast on liberating grace. We are called to feast on being vulnerable before the other so we can risk new and wholesome ways of being in the world. We need to feast on an authentic encounter with the other that exposes who we really are. Exposing our need of the other person – being vulnerable in that need – may be one of the most liberating graces we ever encounter.

We thus become "softer" people because we have encountered our hardness through the acceptance of the other. Our weaknesses become our strengths, and we become salt and light for others: we flavour and experience their lives, as well as our own, in a different way. We thus become freer people: more loving, more faithful to our commitments, humbler, more transparent, less judgmental. We grow in our capacity for intimacy. We grow in empathy, which allows us to live with the sin of the other as a blessing, just as we experience our own sin as a gateway. Indeed, sin *is* a blessing, one which helps us know ourselves more truthfully, as people originally blessed by God.

Questions for Prayerful Reflection

1. What do you identify as sin in your life? This is not a matter of merely identifying your sins. Rather, it asks you to identify the blessings you have stretched to the point where relationships have broken down – relationships with self, with God, with others and with the planet. Name two or three things you have done that demonstrate these breakdowns. These are your sins, for which you will need to seek forgiveness when the time is right.

2. After identifying recent sinful acts or behaviours, can you take a small step to prevent them from happening again? Name this step or steps. Imagine yourself taking them. Identify what it feels like to seek change, restitution or forgiveness.

3. Where do you experience unfreedom in your life? Where do you long to be free? For example, do you overindulge in food or alcohol, do you criticize your partner uncharitably, or did you do something in the past that still bothers you? Name these honestly in your heart and ask God to give you the grace to change or to deal with the issue, even in some small way.

4. Do you believe you are fully aware of how you operate in the world: for example, your attitudes toward others, your habits, your idiosyncrasies? Spend a few moments asking God to enlighten you to any blindness you have in your life. These are the areas you might consider fasting from to see how your quality of life changes for the better.

Meditation Fourteen

The Cross as the Central Symbol of Christian Faith

Companion of the Meditation: Saint Óscar Romero
(1917–1980)

Óscar Romero, a Salvadoran bishop, lived during a time of great political and civil turbulence in El Salvador. Decades of oppression of the poor by the rich and successive corrupt governments went largely unnoticed by the rest of the world. The Salvadoran Army, under the instruction of the corrupt Salvadoran government, killed or abducted protesters who sought reform. The local Catholic Church, regrettably, did little to quell the suffering of its people. Romero, in the earliest part of his episcopacy (he was ordained bishop in 1970) and like the bishops around him, fell into this space of complacency. Remarkably, all of this radically changed for Romero. In 1977, a close priest friend of Romero's was shot and killed along with a child and an elderly man. Romero took this event to heart. He changed from an introverted conservative to an outspoken champion of his people. Romero soon became beloved throughout the Americas as the "voice of the voiceless." In the end, he gave his all to become the face of God for his own people but also for those across Latin America and now the whole world. Members of the Salvadoran Army shot him in the heart on March 24, 1980, while he celebrated Mass in a hospital chapel. Romero was a mystic who became a martyr and saint.[24]

With the apostle Paul, we can proclaim Christ crucified as the central event of our lives. The cross is the core symbol of Christian faith. With Paul we can proclaim:

> When I came to you, brothers and sisters, I did not come proclaiming the mystery of God to you in lofty words or wisdom. For I decided to know nothing among you except Jesus Christ, and him crucified. And I came to you in weakness and in fear and in much trembling. My speech and my proclamation were not with plausible words of wisdom, but with a demonstration of the Spirit and of power, so that your faith might rest not on human wisdom but on the power of God. (1 Corinthians 2:1-5)

In this meditation, we hold in sharp focus the symbol of the cross as demonstrated in the life of Óscar Romero. It could be said that Jesus continues to be crucified in what happened to the Salvadoran people and to Romero himself. Generally, Christ is crucified through tragic events in our own lives, through the persecution of peoples around the globe, and through miscarriages of justice and ill treatment of immigrants and other minorities.

But let's zero in on the dynamics of individual suffering and how they represent Jesus on the cross. As we more closely resemble the person of Jesus in attitude, knowledge and action, we are transformed. Transformative moments of our lives engage us in the cross of Jesus. How ironic that the symbol of such brutality and pain would become for us *the symbol* of Christianity.

The crucifix – not a symbol of the Last Supper or of the empty tomb – is the most widely displayed symbol in places of both private prayer and public worship. Why? The cross conveys the depth of who we are in faith: a people who live for the other in self-giving sacrificial love. The cross is the door that brings us to touch the most profound mystery of who we are as Christians – the mystery of our birth, our life and our death.

Even stylized or decorative crucifixes carried in pomp in our churches cannot hide the horror of the one who died so brutally. The seeming absence of love that frames the cross portrays the most painful death of all. A life without love is tragic enough, but to be abandoned on the brink of death is unimaginable.

I still remember the crucifix hanging in a prominent place in our family's living room when I was a child. Adorned with last year's palm branches, it always seemed dusty and dark, no matter how well lit the room. The annual renewal of the palms woven around the cross on Palm Sunday gave it a momentary resurgence, but eventually the new palm curled and faded, and the shadows again took hold.

Before the cross in places of worship, in private homes and at times in public places, countless people have contemplated the mystery of Jesus throughout the 2,000-year history of

Christianity. This symbol unites us with every one of them. Through the cross, we are made one with all who feel their lives are empty of meaning or who feel abandoned, as Jesus did in his final moments. We could all likely describe times when we felt this way: times when we felt outside the group and did not belong, when our best friend deserted us, when a relationship was breaking down, when tragedy struck and life seemed unbearable, when we have felt unjustly accused.

We must enter these realities as we contemplate the cross of Jesus – the seeming hopelessness of life at various times, or perhaps even right now. The cross is not meant to provide comfort. It is a symbol that leads to sober thought and recollection. It causes us to take stock of our lives while standing in solidarity with the one who died out of love for us. From this perspective, we embrace our experiences and allow them to be illuminated by the crucifixion. This is what guided Romero as he embraced the crosses of his own life and those of the Salvadoran people.

Through the cross, Romero saw how love can conquer all that needs healing in our lives and in our world. Embracing the cross means allowing ourselves to suffer the consequences of our broken humanity without perpetuating the brokenness that brought us to the cross in the first place. That is Jesus' example. He invites us to do the same for others. Love does conquer all, but first we must unconditionally embrace our shared humanity. When we do this, we can forgive, we feel we belong, we extend the benefit of the doubt, and we love the other. Jesus looked beyond the sins of those who placed him on the cross, and he invites us to do the same for those who cause us to suffer. Ironically, this can lead us to a deep sense of joy.

Romero did not call his people to pain and anguish as he preached non-violence in the face of brutal persecution. Rather, he offered a joy-filled invitation to suffer – to embrace with openness – the common good and choose what we can contribute to it. The suffering he speaks of forces us to make daily decisions about how to live the freedom of the cross. Christian life is not built on a set of beliefs recorded in books, proclamations or texts, but on the ability to live with joy in both the shadow of the cross and the light of the empty tomb.

Death and life go hand in hand. But we must not rush quickly past the cross to the resurrection. They go together. We need to feel comfortable embracing the messiness of life – the consequences of human frailty, deceit and betrayal. Just as the cross of Jesus made way for the resurrection, our experiences will reveal God's power in the human condition.

Asking questions such as the following can go a long way to help us embrace the cross while living the joy of the resurrection: How can we contribute to other people's growth? How can we understand their needs better and respond to them? What will unite us rather than divide us? Is there something about how I do things that I need to change?

In soul searching on the above questions, we touch the core of our faith; we touch the cross; we touch God. This is the paradox of suffering and joy. Suffering our crosses may lead us to do or see things differently. We will discover new approaches in moments of abiding joy. Although the challenges do not disappear, embracing our crosses opens the door to new life.

We need to believe that Jesus walks with us, especially in times of trouble. Indeed, God is on the cross with us

> ➤ when we realize we missed opportunities that can never be recovered;

> when health problems cause radical changes in our lives;
> when financial concerns seem to overpower us;
> when important friendships falter and perhaps even fail beyond repair;
> when we are unjustly accused;
> in all kinds of intense stress.

In times of trouble, we need to remember Jesus was there first. As he embraced his cross, he transformed its power from destruction and death to opportunities and new life:

> he responded to the violence against him with forgiveness, not hate;
> he did not use aggression to solve conflict;
> he broke down barriers to form community;
> he offered absolute forgiveness for even the most terrible sin;
> he refused to allow a lack of material resources to prevent him from treating others with compassion.

In short, Jesus showed us how to break the cycle of our broken humanity. From the cross he proclaimed through his actions, "The violence stops here. I will not strike back in word or deed." He taught us how to act, even when others hurt us. Jesus always showed generosity, grace and understanding. In the face of sin against him, he always paid forward a legacy of forgiving acceptance and self-giving love. He invites us to stop whatever we are doing and break bread with one another rather than to break each other; to consider the other in their own context, which has its own crosses.

Our troubles and sinful habits, and those of the people around us, may not go away. But with God's help, we will discover a peace and joy deeper than any affliction or sin.

That peace and joy will carry us through. Our actions show whether we believe this to be true. We are called to forgive those we love most, since they have the power to hurt us most. The opposite is also true: we hurt those we love the most when we are unaware of our sinful tendencies.

As Jesus revealed on the cross, our behaviour reveals *who* we believe in and *what* is important to us. Our actions, more than our words, interpret and make visible God alive in our life. God's Word happens. Jesus breaks open God's message into the fullness of light.

Questions for Prayerful Reflection

1. What comes to mind when you reflect on the cross? Has meditation on the cross, Christ crucified, been part of your spirituality in the past? Why or why not? Do you think that will change?

2. What events in your life would you describe as times where you carried your cross? Pick one. Recall the details and spend a few moments in prayerful meditation on it. Does that event have meaning for you today? Has it helped you view your life or yourself differently? Has that struggle or challenge changed you in some way? If so, how?

3. Who do you hold close in your life and who has hurt you in the past such that you have never been able to forgive? This is a cross in your life. What steps might you take to offer forgiveness?

4. Which person close to you have you hurt and not yet offered an apology? This is a cross in your life. Why are you
unable to apologize? What small step might you take toward
eventually offering that apology?

Meditation Fifteen

Justice-Making: The Face of God in the World

Companion of the Meditation: Saint Marie de l'Incarnation, Mother of Canada (1599–1672)

Born Marie Guyart in the town of Tours, France, her religious name "Marie de l'Incarnation" reminds us of the gift of the Trinity – God become flesh in the person of Jesus Christ through the power of the Holy Spirit. Married at the age of seventeen, Marie gave birth to a son a year later. But she was soon to be widowed. The child was barely a year old when her husband died, leaving Marie to take over the management of his struggling silk business. A single parent who lived at a time when women did not involve themselves in the affairs of business, she knew what it was to face the challenges of life. But she desired to emulate the strong women of the gospels, and that she did. When her son was twelve, she joined the contemplative Ursuline sisters but longed to be a missionary. This desire eventually took her to Canada at the age of forty. She landed in Quebec in 1639 and set out to devote the rest of her life to the service of young girls – both Indigenous and French. The Holy Spirit guided her to bring them a much-needed education; she also guided them in the joys of life through song and dance.[25]

🍂

The prophet Isaiah speaks to us of the future house of God – a house that will be established "as the highest of the mountains … above the hills." (2:1-5) Many people will be attracted to this house, he goes on to say, and they will journey from far and wide to go there. The house of God has special qualities, the greatest of which is its place as a house of justice.

In God's house, swords shall be fashioned into ploughshares, and spears will become garden tools. Violence will have no place here. What Isaiah describes is the essential quality of God's home, that of peace and right relationship, where all people share equally in the goods found there. Where does God live, according to Isaiah? Clearly the prophet is not describing a physical place or building, but a relationship that God wishes to share with all people. The essential quality of this relationship is justice, and it is founded on living in peace and right relationship – now.

This is the nature of Isaiah's prophecy. And it is the nature of the life Marie de l'Incarnation set out to live with the Indigenous and non-Indigenous people of the fledgling territory that would become Canada. She had one word for this prophecy: "love." "Love is my name and I want you to call me thus. People give me many names; but none please me more and expresses better what I am towards them than that one."[26]

Marie de l'Incarnation understood that prophecy is not a telling of the future, but of how things are now and how they should be. Prophecy makes transparent the truth of our living.

In faith, this transparency reveals who we are before God and before one another.

The first receiver of a prophetic word given by God is the one who speaks it. The first receiver of a prophetic word is the first to be responsible for making that prophetic word real in his or her own life. Beware the one who believes that he or she speaks a word of truth "for others": the truth is first a call to examine one's own life to see how one is living that truth. Isaiah received the word of justice; he worked to make that word real for himself and for others. Marie always spoke a word of truth for others in bringing them the justice of a loving God.

Justice-making is the essential characteristic of what God desires for us. Justice – understood as right relationship – which we share with a wide range of individuals, groups and communities, can be lived in different ways. It does not fall from the sky but is intentionally made.

From a secular perspective, John Rawls, a celebrated American philosopher, describes justice as "giving people the ability to realize their potential in the society where they live."[27] In this view, justice must engage the realms of, for example, education, access to health care, a living wage, equality in the workplace and equal access to opportunities. All these are necessary, from Rawls' perspective, to the realization of justice. People need all these to realize their potential and live fully as human beings. A just society is necessary so all can develop personally and professionally, live with happiness and meaning and, in turn, contribute to the lives of others. However, Rawls' notion of justice is built on the idea that one's interest in the life of others is motivated by concern for one's own. It is a self-serving interest dictated by the laws of societies. What more can be brought forth from what Isaiah speaks of and from what Marie de l'Incarnation lived? Something deeper: self-giving sacrificial care, the sanctity of human life and the dignity of all people.

All human life has a dignity rooted in God's dignity. Human laws cannot realize the full potential of justice and equality for all. A full sharing in God's life grounds the cry for justice and equality. Human laws that dictate the sharing of goods, the equality of peoples, and the norms under which people and nations are in relationship with each other only go so far. Sometimes societies establish unjust or oppressive laws. Human nature is ambiguous; we can get caught up in amassing goods and power that ultimately enslave rather than enabling the other to realize their dignity. God models how to overcome our inability to enter fully into justice and equality for all. The model of this type of relationship is the Trinity.

As the persons of the Trinity share life among themselves such that harmony, self-giving love and genuine community emerge, so too must we. The way we share life with others witnesses to God's way of being in relationship. God's grace and empowering Spirit accompany us along the way, since we cannot achieve these goals on our own.

Helping realize the potential of each person and being in right relationship with them are not optional. We will be held accountable for how much, or how little, we contribute to this effort. Many biblical texts proclaim this vision of justice. For example, the prophet Amos admonishes his people for trampling on the needy, trading dishonestly in the marketplace and making greedy business transactions. (Amos 8:4-7)

Here we have the story of a conniving people rubbing their hands with glee at the thought of profit. But the text ends on a solemn note: the Lord says, "I will never forget their deeds."

This text reminds us of justice-making and accountability as reflected in the house of God. God assures us, through the voice of Amos, that we will be held accountable for what we do and what we fail to do.

This is brought into focus in the story Jesus tells about the dishonest manager. (Luke 16:1-13) This story ends in a surprising way. A manager had poorly managed his master's property and had not treated people well. When he was challenged to account for what he had done, he turned over a new leaf. He began treating his master's clients fairly and honestly. The master noticed this and commended the dishonest manager for acting so shrewdly. The manager had learned to be accountable and to act justly.

Perhaps the manager did not deserve this recognition: after all, he had a change of heart only because his master had discovered his dishonest ways. But how are we to know his motives? How are we to know the motivation behind our own actions and choices? Even the most splendid of our choices stem from both noble and less noble reasons. Our motives are never so pure that we are beyond reproach. We always make choices with several points of reference.

The story of the shrewd manager provides an example of an outcome that is not what we might expect or even hope for in the stories of Jesus. Logic might have had us conclude that the master should have punished the manager for trying to buy his favour. But the story does not take that direction. In a similar way, God continually challenges what we consider to be God's ways in the world. In the case of the unjust manager, we are surprised to see justice delivered in an unusual way. God uses even our impure motives and less than noble reasons to accomplish what is right and just. Even our sinful lives can be instruments of God's care and concern.

Living in God's house requires transformational change that is political, economic and societal. We can invest our time and resources in these changes so every person is treated with equal dignity and enabled to develop their full potential. But another level of justice-making needs consideration: the personal, transformative side. Justice must be exercised in our personal lives: with others and with ourselves.

How are we naturally held accountable for the responsibilities and commitments we accept? How do we make justice in the less formal parts of our lives? Relationships – and corresponding commitments – arise through friendships, volunteer efforts, family life or even when we experience poor health or experience dramatic or tragic change in our lives. Through these relationships, we can help ourselves and others realize our full potential together. All of these situations call forth our ability to nurture right relationships. Have we used well what has been given to us to do this?

In all our responsibilities, we can make small and large efforts to help. Let's be cunning and wise about it like the "dishonest" manager. We all have the potential to make justice within our responsibilities and accountabilities, whether they are large or small. We always need to look for ways we can improve in right relationship, in justice-making.

. . . .

Questions for Prayerful Reflection

1. Think of some deed or choice you have made in your life – one that particularly pleased you. What prompted you to make that choice or perform that act? Were your motives pure and noble, without hope for personal recognition? Were you totally self-divested of the hope for personal gain?

2. Do you need to leave the comfort of your current situation to risk new ways for justice-making? What boundaries do you need to cross to be better positioned to realize more fully the potential for your own life? What does the space between here and there feel like?

3. What would it mean to be generous with yourself at this time in your life? To be generous with others?

4. How are you naturally held accountable for your responsibilities and commitments at home and at work? How do you make justice when it comes to the responsibilities given to you in the less formal parts of your life? In your workplace?

5. What emotional terrain must you wade into to better understand justice-making? Do you need to change some attitudes to become better at justice-making?

Meditation Sixteen

Discerning God's Presence in Every Day

Companion of the Meditation: Patron Saint of Children: Nicholas of Myra (270–343)

The widespread popularity of this saint is obvious from the many churches built in his honour. Nicholas is said to have been a bishop of the ancient Greek city of Myra, by the sea. He was known for his holiness and faith. His parents apparently died at a young age, leaving him financially comfortable. He made a commitment to himself to use his inheritance for works of charity. There is a story that he over three days, three times he threw a bag of gold into an impoverished man's house under the cloak of night as a dowry for the man's three daughters – the man was going to give his daughters over to prostitution because he had no dowry to offer potential suitors. Although Nicholas died in Myra, his remains were transported to Bari, Italy, in 1087, where they remain. Many miracles were attributed to him. He is said to have been portrayed by Christian artists more often than any other saint except Mary, the mother of Jesus. The legend of the three bags of gold for the three children gave rise to his patronage of children, especially in Germany, Switzerland and the Netherlands. Gifts were given to children in his name at Christmas. This custom was popularized by Dutch Protestants who immigrated to America. They converted the Catholic saint into a Nordic magician (Santa Claus = Sint Klae = Saint Nicholas), who delights boys and girls all over the world at Christmas.

In the First Book of Samuel (3:3-10) we meet the boy Samuel, who was about twelve years old. While Samuel was with the high priest, Eli, he heard someone calling to him three times one night. Like many of us, Samuel did not realize it was the Lord calling him. Three times, Samuel heard a voice; each time he went to Eli to see what he wanted. Even Eli, despite his advanced years and wisdom, took time to figure out what was happening. Eventually, Eli instructed Samuel that if he heard the voice again he should reply, "your servant is listening."

Take this Bible story to heart. We have the capacity to "hear" God in everyday events, but we often fail to hear God or to believe that God can speak to us personally. Yet we were created with "ears" that can hear God's voice. We have a natural desire for God and, if we pay attention to this, it can lead us toward a fulfilling and meaningful life. However, this inner awareness of God's presence needs to be trained to hear God. Our everyday experiences speak to us and make us aware that God is accompanying us – in making difficult decisions as well as in everyday life.

When I went to teach English at a high school in Haiti, I made a two-year commitment. A few months after arriving, I discovered that I didn't want to be there. By the ninth month, my whole being was in revolt. I prayed about this often, but I can't say that I heard the voice of God. Surprisingly, soon after those first nine months, I felt in my bones the most authentic response to the situation I could ever have imagined: a great sense of peace settled into my being. It was as if God was saying, "Stay a while longer with me." It still wasn't easy, but it felt right. It took some time to listen and let emerge the most authentic response I could make. Eventually, God's response came in the feeling of peace.

What experiences have you had when you listened to the core of your bones? If we find it difficult to hear God speak, perhaps we should recall our youth, when we were about the same age as Samuel. Perhaps we were less cynical about life, about others and about ourselves. These were our "child days" – a time (not necessarily measured by our age) before grudges have built up and wounds clouded our perspective.

Like the children Saint Nicholas visited on the feast day of the birth of Jesus, we may need to return to a time when we were firmly in the embrace of promise and hope, awe and wonder, when we were attuned to the great possibilities of life. Children are trusting, spontaneous, creative and daring. It is to them that Jesus promises the kingdom of heaven: "Truly I tell you, unless you change and become like little children, you will never enter the kingdom of heaven." (Matthew 18:3) Having the attitude of a child can open our capacity to discern God's presence.

Children allow their parents to do what they cannot do for themselves; this is the kind of relationship God longs to establish with each of us. Jesus describes this relationship because it is the kind he shares with God. Jesus does not act alone but is continually in communion with God. He depends on

God, allowing God to do with him as God wills. Jesus drinks the cup that God gives him and entrusts his life to God. This awareness and deep faith are what gave Jesus hope and support in his journey. He invites us also to rely on God.

But sometimes these wellsprings of hope and promise are buried by the challenges, disappointments and betrayals of life. We may pile high our past troubles, setbacks and deceptions, and lean on them for a while. It is easy to blame them for our current malaise – for our lack of capacity to experience God and be happy. But eventually, we must let go of all these things and let God take on all that we cannot.

We can even become deaf and blind to our "child days" by untrue assumptions about other people, ways in which we may have been offended and talents we simply do not possess. A lack of self-awareness can be a major block to experiencing God's presence in our daily experiences. We are created in the image and likeness of God; to get in touch with the image within is to get in touch with the truth of our lives. God is Truth; Truth will set us free.

We may hold a toxic and untrue image of God: that God is waiting to catch us in a moment of weakness, that God is "a preying God" instead of "a praying God." We need to let go of these images, for they may lead to untruths about ourselves and our lives. If our images of God do not lead us to compassion, self-appreciation and conversion, they are false images of God. They result in a false sense of self and lead to the inability to experience the presence of God. Many of us see the world not as it is, but as we are – broken and alone. But this is not the truth of our lives. God cannot work with phonies but only with the real and the true.

If we cannot let go of our untruths, we will find ourselves in a self-constructed prison of duplicity and silence. Everyday experiences become impenetrable to God's abiding presence; tragically, we do not experience God's deep care. We become victims of the banality and deceit of our lives, feeling that God is far away when, in fact, God is hovering beside us, above us, below us, waiting for us to hear, to see and to feel God's abiding presence.

Ignatius of Loyola, a sixteenth-century Spanish mystic and saint, developed a method to help followers of Jesus understand themselves better and to become aware of the presence of God in their lives. He called this method, practised daily, an *examination of conscience* or an "examination of self-awareness." Ignatius knew that if we become more knowledgeable about what we are feeling and thinking, and more aware of what happened during our day, we will come to know how God speaks through the events of our lives. Essentially, Ignatius taught his followers three things to help them be attuned to God's presence: *be aware* of what happened, understand and *reflect* on what happened, and then *decide* on steps forward.

Here is a simple method to pray daily these three moments:

Find a comfortable spot where distractions will be minimized. Notice your body. Notice your breathing. Become aware of the love with which God looks upon you. Ask for honest insight. Review your day with God. Stay where something stands out. Give thanks to God for all that is good. Ask for forgiveness and healing where you need it. Pray the Lord's Prayer.

As we get closer to God and accomplish what God is calling us to, we enter a state of happiness that does not depend on the ups and downs of life. Even in extreme adversity we can experience this deep-seated happiness and be joyful. In this place of happiness, our life spontaneously opens up to include others, so that the truth of our life may also be theirs.

True happiness is not dependent on what is happening outside of us: it is the result of what is happening within. In listening to and accepting what is of God in everyday life and rejecting what is not, we hear God and can be led to an abiding joy, peace and happiness, even when things get rough.

God is never offended by our humanity, for through that humanity God speaks to us and we come to know God, others and ourselves better. We also learn to be patient with the humanity of others. We never know what is happening in the heart of another, how God is quietly and patiently guiding the other along. We are there to encourage and support, not judge and tear down. God cannot stop giving of Godself in the ordinary moments of daily life. But we ought not to spend too much time analyzing our life: analysis can cause paralysis. Noticing, understanding better and acting accordingly should not be a chore.

We trust in God's quiet presence, and we listen for it. If, after some time, our examination of consciousness does not lead to peace and a sense of well-being, then perhaps we should consider doing things differently. Let God be God in our lives, take a step back and trust that we can be alive to the everyday when we see with the eyes of faith. God's presence is fresh every day. A Buddhist saying can be instructive for us: "Enter each day with a beginner's mind." God's presence is a surprise with each new dawn.

. . . .

Questions for Prayerful Reflection

1. Recall a period when your life seemed especially happy and meaningful. What events were occurring at that time? Do you attribute your happiness to these events? Were you aware of how God appeared in those events? Why or why not?

2. Recall a time when your life seemed difficult and problematic. What events were occurring then? Do you attribute your despair to these events? Were you aware of how God was guiding you then? Why or why not?

3. Take a few minutes to understand better what was occurring in your faith life in the scenarios explored in questions 1 and 2. In either or both scenarios, is there anything you would accept as being of God or reject as counterproductive to the fullness of life to which God calls you?

4. Recall a few events in your life from the past week or so. Might any of them reveal how God is speaking to you now? Choose one of them to become aware, understand better and embrace – follow it through to deeper meaning with the eyes of faith.

Meditation Seventeen

Did Jesus Tell Jokes?
The Humour of God

. . . .

Companion of the Meditation: Patron Saint
of Comedians, Dancers and Actors: Vitus (c. 290–c. 303)

Vitus lived at a difficult time in Christian history. The Roman emperor Diocletian had issued an edict to remove the legal rights of Christians so they would leave Christianity and worship the gods of the Roman Empire. Vitus, born in Sicily, refused to denounce his Baptism, which he requested when he was seven or eight years old. At the time, he did not tell his parents of his decision to be baptized. A devout Christian, he was martyred by the Roman authorities when he was thirteen. In the late Middle Ages in some parts of Europe, the feast of Saint Vitus was celebrated by dancing before his statue. He came to be recognized as the patron saint of dancers, comedians and actors. The remains of Saint Vitus are entombed in a church in the state of Saxony in eastern Germany.

"Humor is a prelude to faith, and laughter is the beginning of prayer." Reinhold Niebuhr

We don't easily associate the Christian life with humour, laughter, play or comedy.[28] But if we were to ask ourselves to name the characteristics of another person we would like to know or who we find attractive, we would likely include humour among their personality traits. In admonishing someone, we may say, "Don't take yourself too seriously." We are telling the person that life has a lighter side. We come into this world with an instinct to laugh. Think of all the smiling babies who break into laughter for no evident reason. We all laughed before we spoke a single word.

Humour finds its way into our preferences and our relationships in several ways. But appreciating humour as a spiritual virtue – a virtue that can enrich our faith life with God and each other – can be a challenge. Unfortunately, Luke's Gospel appears to warn against laughter: "Woe upon you who laugh now; you shall mourn and weep." (Luke 6:25)

God is portrayed elsewhere in the Bible as laughing, but the results are not friendly:

The kings of the earth set themselves, and the rulers take counsel together,
against the LORD and his anointed, saying,
"Let us burst their bonds asunder, and cast their cords from us."
He who sits in the heavens laughs; the LORD has them in derision.
Then he will speak to them in his wrath and terrify them in his fury. (Psalm 2:2-5)

The *Rule of St. Benedict* explicitly forbade monks from laughing. Saint Benedict, who lived in the fourth century, instructed his monks: "Not to love much talking; not to speak useless words or words that move to laughter; not to love much or boisterous laughter."[29] Saint John Chrysostom, also in the fourth century, went so far as to say that tears resulting from reflection on our sins bring us closer to God than laughter does.

Yet, down through the ages, laughter and comedy were sometimes seen as integral to the Christian life. For example, in Germany during the sixteenth century, Catholic priests would tell jokes during their Easter homily. The goal was to laugh at Satan, who had been defeated by the resurrection.

However, the stronger tradition of not seeing humour, laughter, comic behaviour, the telling of jokes, clever plays on words, stand-up comedy and the like as contributing to Christian faith life has continued until our own time. But is there good reason for this? Shouldn't Christian living include laughter and levity? Vitus danced before the tabernacle much as King David did in the Old Testament. Christians understood that their relationship with God gave rise to laughter, joy and happiness. Perhaps a way to realize God did indeed laugh, and so should we, is to ask, "Did Jesus tell jokes?" We take ourselves seriously, but Jesus didn't do the same himself.

Indeed, Jesus displayed a sense of humour that was key to the message he preached about the Reign of God. Even the choice of the all-powerful God to take on the fragility of human flesh in Jesus is comic. Jesus spent the bulk of his life as an ordinary worker, a labourer in a carpenter shop. He seems to have enjoyed the merriment of many social gatherings, to the point that he provided more wine when it ran out at a wedding.

And, after his resurrection, he showed a sense of humour in revealing himself first to a woman, Mary Magdalene. In those days, women were considered second-class citizens. Ordinary labourer, partygoer and friend of second-class citizens – a degree of humour exists in these stories and others like them in the gospels.

But we do not live in first-century Palestine. We don't always get the humour in Jesus' parables, his actions and the way he encountered people, because humour is culturally conditioned. Furthermore, it is possible that first-century writers recording stories about Jesus edited out some explicit humorous actions of Jesus to present the gospel as "serious business." The writers were, after all, launching a movement that the Roman authorities persecuted.

Yet the people surrounding Jesus would have laughed at his exaggerated and ridiculous illustrations. The idea that someone would light a lamp and put it under a bushel basket (Matthew 5:14-16) or build a house on sand (Matthew 7:26), or even that with a little faith you could move mountains (Matthew 17:20), would have been comic examples for his listeners. In these examples, Jesus does not use mockery or sarcasm to put people down to incite laughter: he uses the novel and the ironic to bring forth his message and make people smile. Jesus' humour is warm and affectionate. He uses it to bring his followers, as well as others, closer to him. We miss much of the humour Jesus would have intended because we see the world from the viewpoint of the twenty-first century. Jesus lived in a time and place foreign to us, but that doesn't mean we can't appreciate his sense of humour by better understanding the time in which he lived. He showed the importance of humour.

When it is carefully inserted into a situation, humour can dissipate tension, ease stress or break the ice to get people talking to one another. Humour can be the beginning of authentic relationships and communitarian living – thus, the importance of humour in the development of our spirituality. As Christians, we have many ways to bond. Humour, laughter and joy are all part of healthy Christian living.

When humorously engaged with others, we feel more a part of the community. Authentic humour produces no winners or losers, but only respectful fun that deepens our feeling of belonging to a group, growing in closeness to others and becoming aware of our own identity.

Of course, we also have experienced the other side of humour, where it is used to mock or sarcastically attack others. That is not humour at all. Rather, it shows disrespect for and diminishment of the other. Genuine humour is not malicious. If what we try to pass off as humour does not bring people together, then it is not humour but scorn and belittling of the other.

Humour ought not to violate another person's dignity. A balance needs to be achieved between provoking a light-hearted chuckle and the denigration of the other.

If we find ourselves laughing at others too often and not laughing with them, we may need to check how we are using humour. What is taking place? Are we deploying true humour, or are we subtly putting down the other by our own statements or by laughing in support of another person's malicious commentary?

Using stereotypes as the basis for comic relief can also be damaging. We might think we can excuse ourselves by saying, "I'm just joking," but the one against whom the so-called comic slight is directed may not be easily convinced. God's humour is not harmful or racist or sexist. God's humour does not support prejudice, intolerance or injustice toward another human being or a community.

If a sudden turn of events causes someone to be different in some way and we laugh at them instead of showing empathy, we need to reflect on what is causing our laughter. Is there an implicit puffing up of our own selves? Does our laughter say, "I'm better than that. Ha-ha!"? We may try to disguise our chuckle – or worse, outright laughter – but it will be too late. The "innocence" of our laughter may have painfully humiliated or embarrassed the other, creating a barrier in our relationship. We see this in the children's mockery and jeering against the prophet Elisha. (2 Kings 2:23) When a large group of children laughed at the prophet for his baldness, Elisha cursed them, and then two bears came out of the woods and mauled forty-two of the children. No wonder laughter received a bad rap in the early church!

As the recipient of someone else's "humour," we may find ourselves feeling bad and diminished. In this case we may need to check in with ourselves. Do we allow ourselves to be subjected to destructive barbs coming our way? Maybe we need to say "enough is enough" and address the situation. We may ask ourselves, "Is the other person using 'humour' to put me down and help them feel more important?" It takes courage to deal with these situations in the moment, but sometimes it is necessary if we are to retain our sense of well-being.

Humour can give life to the soul. It can strengthen our tolerance for difference and ambiguity (not everybody sees the world as we do), help us appreciate ourselves in new ways (and not be overly sensitive), break the ice in new relationships and start a conversation. Joy, humour and laughter are spiritual gifts we can nurture, much as we can develop forgiveness, generosity and prayer. They all take practice. If used properly, humour is a lubricant for relationships. The pleasure experienced in humour is what binds us together in our humanity. Joy and happiness attract. The language of laughter can unite us as one.

> Lord, I know that you have a sense of Humor.
> You used to smile, in fact you used to laugh out loud...
> Give me the gift of humor, teach me to smile and to
>   laugh.
> This is the gift which gives consolation,
>   encouragement, dynamic force...
> Give me all this, for myself and for the other people
>   as well. Amen.[30]

. . . .

Questions for Prayerful Reflection

1. When was the last time you engaged in solid laughter, a genuine, deep belly laugh? Take a moment to recall what drew you into that moment.

2. What role, if any, does humour play in your faith life? Why?

3. Think of an example when you used humour. What role did it play in that situation (for example, divide, bring together, act as an ice-breaker, lessen tension or add to the celebration)?

4. Can you think of an example when "humour" was directed at you in an unfriendly way? How did this make you feel? Were you able to tell the other person how you felt? Why or why not?

5. Can you think of a time when you used humour to put down another person? Describe what you did and what it led to.

6. How might you make humour more a part of your faith life?

Meditation Eighteen

The Journey Travelled: The Quest to Live Symbolically

....

Companion of the Meditation: Patron Saint of Art and Against Temptations: Catherine of Bologna (1413–1463)

From an early age, Catherine felt the tug of God on her heart. Her father was a lawyer and diplomat, occupations that afforded the family the resources to educate Catherine. Her father died when Catherine had barely entered her teens. But she seized that moment to join a group of semi-monastic Franciscans. Her devotion to religious life was admirable, but within it she experienced many trials as well as graces in the form of visions from God. Her work in the monastery was simple: baker, laundress, dressmaker and tender of the animals. She provided for the daily sustenance of the community in many ways and rejoiced in this work. Later, she was given the responsibility of overseeing the young women joining the community. Catherine went on to establish a new monastery called the Convent of Corpus Christi, where her holiness revealed itself in powers of healing and prophecy. During her free time, she copied her prayer book, illuminating it with colours and vivid images. She also painted miniatures that drew great praise for their artistry. Women painters, especially nuns, were rare at the time. Catherine, practical to the core, left three simple rules by which to live: first, always speak well of others; second, be humble; third, don't meddle in others' business. Her incorrupt body may still be viewed in the convent church in Bologna, Italy.

You have reached the final meditation. In reading these pages, you have made a journey. Do you have a sense of where you started in this journey? Where have you travelled through these meditations? Where are you going? What have the meditations in this book meant to you: in your personal life, your family life, your professional life and your community engagement (friends and volunteering)? It is an ongoing journey, with new vistas always opening before us.

When you set out, you cast your net, trusting that Jesus will feed you as he fed the communities of people that followed him. When you feel you don't have enough, you need to meditate on Matthew's words and remember that an abundance was left over. We are always given the food we need for our journey. By reflecting on our lives, circumstances and resources, we can see how this is true: not merely as an intellectual affirmation, but as a felt response to the presence of God in our hearts.

We have come to understand that by living in Jesus, we live Trinitarian life. We are followers of the Way, which is Trinitarian – the life of the fullness of God as exemplified in Jesus and which the Holy Spirit has brought to us as a gift. This makes us disciples of the Reign of God – God's way of being in the world – with all the mystery that goes into living that Reign as people of faith.

As baptized members of that Reign, we were ushered into God's life in a unique way. But that is not the only way the Reign of God is accomplished in the world. The breadth and depth of God's Reign is too rich to be fully captured in one cultural or historical moment. Like a prism turning in the sun, the Reign of God lights up the full range of human potential enlivened by God across the ages. Our Baptism began our journey in God's life in earnest: at first through our parents or guardians. Over the years, we accepted this call personally.

That call is sustained through the myriad forms of prayer that Christians have developed across the centuries and through a range of traditions. Prayer – living life with God – is a necessary part of Christian life. We ought to pray daily. Prayer is habitual mindfulness that our existence depends on God's abiding presence. We are not an orphaned people but are accompanied in every moment by a God who cannot help but be present to us. God is present in our sin and fears, in joy and celebration. What a marvellous and faithful companion our God is!

Our life in God is an enfleshed life. This flesh, this body, this life, nourishes us and others. Our bodies are holy ground – a source of God's incarnational presence in the world for others. As God loved human flesh through the person of Jesus, we too are loved and called to love others. The Incarnation is the powerful witness to this truth. God risked everything to undertake this journey of love, and so should we.

In the person of Jesus, God took the definitive step to provide an authentic witness to how God is present in the world – not in positions of authority, privileged decision making or wealth, but from heartfelt concern for all people. How blessed this is! That heartfelt concern is a sign we are on the path to being part of the Reign of God. It is our experience of the cross. We do not seek suffering for its own sake. Rather, we experience the cross in

- › the transformation of hate to provide care for others;
- › the elimination of aggression to bring about peace;
- › the toppling of barriers to form community;
- › the acknowledgement that all have equal access to the resources of the earth, to eliminate hunger and poverty at all levels;
- › the acceptance that we are people who need reconciliation and forgiveness.

In embracing the crosses of our lives and recalling the frightened disciples who left Jerusalem to go to Emmaus after the crucifixion, we turn back from our journey to Emmaus; we return to Jerusalem to continue our journey with the crucified and risen Christ. In this way we express incarnational love, which always challenges and subverts the status quo of our lives.

In Jerusalem we are at the service of God's people. Justice-making is central to this service. The equality of all people is a cornerstone of what we stand for. But we need to be shrewd about this, like the dishonest manager in Matthew's Gospel. We give our all in this effort, just as God gave God's all in the life, death and resurrection of Jesus.

When we feel we have nothing left to offer, we have arrived exactly where God wants us – at a self-emptying that calls to mind the kenosis of Jesus on the cross. This brings us full circle to the life to which we committed ourselves in Baptism. In this emptiness God finds the perfect place to call home. The Paschal Mystery is at the heart of the cross we embrace. God is on the cross with us so we can experience the fullness of the resurrection. To live this life, we cannot simply plot a path that will guide us harmoniously from the first point through to the end, from birth to death. We will follow many convoluted pathways. That is why we need to learn to live symbolically, as did Catherine of Bologna.

Living symbolically means we call upon our creative abilities to imagine words, choices and beliefs that will break open the present moment to the full depth of meaning. We cannot live merely in our heads, stuffed with concepts, knowledge and facts. Our spiritual self is best engaged through artistic and imaginative expression. In short, our imaginations enable us to live the ways God is breaking into and out of our lives. We each need to be an artist. Catherine of Bologna, as well as in writing, discovered artistic drawing and painting as the medium par excellence to express the creative ways she lived and discovered the God who was intimately engaged in her life.

Artists are creative. They imagine the unimaginable and bring that to light in a wide range of media and practical living. As artists on our own journeys, we seek to find creative ways to bring the mystery that is God into the light of day. We need to find ways to enliven the music of God being played in our lives.

For many of us, this is one of the most difficult challenges of our faith. We simply cannot believe that it is true: God journeying with us? God with me? God shining through me? We are too practical – we live too much in our heads – to believe this could be true. We think that maybe this is true for somebody else, but not for me.

We need to find ways to *not* be practical. Instead, we should seek creative ways to be in touch with, name, embody and express imaginative interior movements that feed us on our journey. We need to find ways to tap into our own imagery: the personal way God comes into our lives.

Some will be better able to touch those imaginative movements than others. But we can all learn how to do it through practising. The richness of our personal expression of God-become-flesh cannot be underestimated. God's embodiment in our lives is precious and life-giving. Paying attention to it will lead us to new ways of naming our experiences of God. Taking time in silence to identify appropriate symbols and images that naturally come to us opens doors to new energy and spirit. Doing this in the context of, for example, praying, listening to music, reading poetry, exploring body movement or walking in nature can be fruitful.

Discover the art that speaks to you: dance, music, mime, storytelling, statuary, visual arts, the art of nature, beautiful architecture and so on. You will know this voice when you experience mystery, awe, peace and happiness as you listen to the art. In paying attention to these feelings, images will arise. From these images new insights can surface when we reflect upon them. Such reflection will allow you to enter more fully into the mystery of your life and explore more readily how God is guiding you.

Getting in touch with your creativity will lead you to share it. Shared creativity is a way for others to participate in our faith journey. Our physical, emotional and imaginative powers, as well as our analytical skills, can move us toward personal and communitarian wholeness in God. We need to come to our senses in expressing our faith. Through these powers we integrate diverse ways of knowing. As Esau says to Jacob in the Book of Genesis:

"Please accept my gift that is brought to you, because God has dealt graciously with me, and because I have everything I want." So he urged him, and he took it. Then Esau said, "Let us journey on our way, and I will go alongside you." (33:11-12)

With Esau and Jacob, we can be assured that God is journeying alongside each of us in our own way.

. . . .

Questions for Prayerful Reflection

1. What kind of artistic expression(s) do you enjoy, that personally engages you? What do you find attractive about this art? Try to be specific in describing your attraction and noting how it opens your sense of awe.

2. Are you an artist? Take a moment to put into words what your art expresses about *you*.

3. When you go about your daily routines, do you ever notice small signs of God's presence – in nature, unexpected turns of events, comments or gestures by other people, scripture readings, sudden thoughts or unexpected insights? How might you go about nurturing your openness to these symbolic communications from God?

4. In reading these pages, you have made a journey. What is that journey? What part of the journey is still to be made so you can tangibly experience the Trinitarian Spirit – God, Jesus and the Holy Spirit?

Remember to download the three additional
meditations that are available online:
en.novalis.ca/20-Minute-Retreat-Extra-Sessions/

Meditation Nineteen: Baptized into Life with God

Companion: Patron Saint of Jurors:
Catherine of Siena

Meditation Twenty: Diminishment and Loss as
Gospel Values

Companion: Patron Saint of Loss of Parents: Edith Stein

Meditation Twenty-One: The Mysticism of Every Day

Companion: Patron Saint of Dairy Workers; Medicine/
Healers: Brigid of Ireland

Endnotes

1   Unless otherwise indicated, brief biographies of the companion saints are from *Butler's Lives of the Saints*, Christian Classics, 4 vols., edited, revised and supplemented by Herbert J. Thurston, s.j. and Donald Attwater (Burns & Oates, 1981). Used with permission.

2   Some text for this meditation is extracted and edited from David B. Perrin, *Studying Christian Spirituality* (New York: Routledge, 2007), 157–76. Used with permission.

3   Teresa of Kolkata, National Prayer Breakfast, Feb. 3, 1994.

4   Some text for this meditation is extracted and edited from Perrin, *Studying Christian Spirituality*, 185–203. Used with permission.

5   Hildegard of Bingen, *Scivias*, Mother Columba Hart and Jane Bishop (trans.) (New York: Paulist, 1990).

6   Catherine of Siena, *The Dialogue*, cited in *Saint Catherine: Passion for Truth, Compassion for Humanity*, Susanne Noffke (trans.), Mary O'Driscoll (ed.), (New York: New City Press, 2008), 113–14.

7   John of the Cross, *Living Flame of Love* in *The Collected Works of Saint John of the Cross*, Revised Edition, K. Kavanaugh and Otilio Rodriguez (trans.), (Washington, DC: ICS Publications, 1991), 646; slightly adapted.

8   John of the Cross, *Living Flame*, 707; slightly adapted.

9   Hildegard, *Scivias*, 418.

10 Hildegard, *Scivias*, II.2.6.

11 William Paul Young, *The Shack: Where Tragedy Confronts Eternity* (Newbury Park, CA: Windblown Media, 2007), 100.

12 Teresa of Avila, *The Interior Castle*, E. Allison Peers (trans.), (New York: Bantam Doubleday Dell, 1990), 181.

13 Thérèse of Lisieux, *Story of a Soul: The Autobiography of St. Thérèse of Lisieux*, 3rd ed., John Clarke, OCD (trans.) (Washington, DC: ICS Publications, 1996), 220.

14 Thérèse of Lisieux, *Story of a Soul*, 196.

15 Cited in Klyne R. Snodgrass, *Who God Says You Are: A Christian Understanding of Identity* (Grand Rapids, MI: Eerdmans, 2018), 134. Snodgrass suggests that this quote, not found in Clare's collected works, is more likely a summation of her thought. See Snodgrass, *Who God Says You Are*, 134, fn. 4.

16 Mechthild von Magdeburg, *The Flowing Light of the Godhead*, cited in Dorothee Soelle, *The Silent Cry: Mysticism and Resistance*, Barbara and Martin Rumscheidt (trans.), (Minneapolis: Fortress Press, 2001), 64.

17 *The Westminster Collection of Christian Prayers*, compiled by Dorothy M. Stewart (London: Westminster John Knox Press, 2002), 336; slightly adapted.

18 Julian of Norwich, *The Revelations of Divine Love of Julian of Norwich*, James Walsh (trans.), (London: Burns and Oates, 1961), 56.

19 Summarized from Meaghen Hale, "Saint Kateri Tekakwitha (1680)," in David Beresford et al. (ed.), *Canadian Saints* (Ottawa, ON: Justin Press, 2015), 133–41, and www.katerishrine.com (accessed September 30, 2018).

20 Some text for this meditation is extracted and edited from Perrin, *Studying Christian Spirituality*, 243–48. Used with permission.

21 Etty Hillesum, *Etty: The Letters and Diaries of Etty Hillesum 1941–1943*, Klaas Smelik (ed.), Arnold Pomerans (trans.), (Ottawa: Novalis, 2002), 71.

22 https://catholicrurallife.org/resources/spiritual/prayers-for-rural-families (accessed May 31, 2019).

23 Augustine of Hippo, *The City of God*, Marcus Dods (trans.), Book XIII, Par 14 (New York: Random House, 1950), 423.

24 Summarized from James R. Brockman (ed. and trans.), *Óscar Romero: The Violence of Love* (Maryknoll, NY: Orbis Books, 2004).

25 Summarized from Anne Boily, "Saint Marie de l'Incarnation (1680)," in David Beresford et al. (ed.), *Canadian Saints* (Ottawa, ON: Justin Press, 2015), 122–32.

26 Revelation of Christ to Marie de l'Incarnation as recorded by Dom Guy-Marie Oury, *Marie de l'Incarnation* (1599-1672), Vol. 1, 83 cited in *Canadian Saints*, 122.

27 This idea is developed in John Rawls, *A Theory of Justice* (Cambridge, MA: The Belkap Press of Harvard University Press, 1971).

28 Resources used for the writing of this meditation: Henri Cormier, *The Humor of Jesus* (New York: Alba House, 1977) and James Martin, SJ, *Between Heaven and Mirth: Why Joy, Humor, and Laughter Are at the Heart of the Spiritual Life* (New York: HarperCollins, 2011).

29 St. Benedict, *St. Benedict's Rule for Monasteries*, Leonard J. Doyle (trans.), (Collegeville, MN: The Liturgical Press, 1948), chapter 4:53–55, p. 16.

30 Cormier, *The Humor of Jesus*, 13.